Seasons of Hope

"Many people in our parish community have become involved with Seasons of Hope. It has brought hope, healing, peace, and love to so many. One of the great aspects of this program is that by offering four 'seasons' our parish can provide multiple opportunities each year for people to participate when they are ready for that first step or return when they are ready for more. Most importantly, Seasons of Hope engages the faith life of those who use it and draws them into a deeper relationship with the living God. What a blessing it has been for our parish!"

Rev. Msgr. Stephen J. Avila
Pastor, St. Joseph, Guardian of the Holy Family Parish
Falmouth, Massachusetts

"What most drew me to Seasons of Hope was its explicitly Catholic foundation. In contrast to secular support groups for the grieving, Seasons of Hope puts Jesus at the center and invites participants to entrust their loss and loneliness to him within the abundant consoling wisdom of our Catholic tradition. Having just lost my mother, I was a natural candidate for Seasons of Hope as a facilitator. Its well-structured format enhanced our efforts and when the sessions came to a close, I'd grown quite attached to my fellow group members. It was hard for all of us to see our time together end."

Bishop Liam Cary
Diocese of Baker, Oregon

"As a seasoned facilitator of MacLeod's marvelous program, time and time again I have witnessed the Holy Spirit at work as participants journey together in and through their grief. They consistently express appreciation for the uniquely faith-based content that may have attracted them to Seasons of Hope in the first place, or that was lacking in other grief support programs some had participated in, or that spoke to them as they sought God's presence and a greater understanding of their grief. For those considering facilitating this program, be assured that the *Leader's Guide* is filled with Donna's insightful, practical, and comprehensive guidance that's sure to bless."

Reen Markland
Parish Nurse, St. Bridget of Ireland Catholic Church
Berryville, Virginia

"Seasons of Hope is a godsend. It is solidly Catholic, imbued by hope and comfort while also being open to the real experiences of each participant. It provides an opportunity for those who are grieving to be together, share what is in their hearts, listen to God and to each other, and be heard and comforted. The program is simple, easy to lead, and scripture based. It gets people through hard times, giving them courage to surrender to God and invite him into their pain, and that this made all the difference."

Anna Loch
Former Outreach Manager, Gardens of Gethsemani Cemetery
Archdiocese of Vancouver, British Columbia

"Our bereavement ministry has been using this program for the last ten years and it always works for us. Donna MacLeod's step-by-step *Leader's Guide* always puts me at ease when leading grief-support meetings. More importantly, this program gives each participant new hope in the Catholic Church and how it can help a hurting person in their grief journey."

Karen Jones
Bereavement Ministry, St. Patrick's Catholic Church
Placerville, California

"Communicating loss is essential. Opportunities to communicate with others are essential. Opportunities to communicate with God are necessary. Seasons of Hope offers those opportunities and, as a bishop, I offer my whole-hearted support and blessing."

From the foreword by **Bishop John P. Dolan**
Diocese of Phoenix

LEADER'S GUIDE

Seasons of Hope

Bringing Comfort through Catholic Grief Support

M. Donna MacLeod

Foreword by Bishop John P. Dolan, Diocese of Phoenix

Ave Maria Press AVE Notre Dame, Indiana

Nihil Obstat: Msgr. Michael Heintz, Ph.D.
Censor Librorum

Imprimatur: Most Reverend Kevin C. Rhoades
Bishop of Ft. Wayne–South Bend
Given at Fort Wayne, Indiana, on August 8, 2023

Founded in 1865, Ave Maria Press is a ministry of the United States Province of Holy Cross.

www.avemariapress.com

Paperback: ISBN-13 978-1-64680-232-6

E-book: ISBN-13 978-1-64680-276-0

Cover and text design by Katherine Robinson.

Printed and bound in the United States of America.

To Erynne Lee MacLeod,
a cherished daughter who loved Jesus
and now lives with him,
and to her dad, my dear husband Bryan,
who has faithfully been by my side
every step of this life-giving ministry.

Contents

Foreword

Everyone dies, and each of us at some point faces the death of a loved one. It is a simple and hard truth. I am not unique in my experiences regarding the loss of loved ones. Although losing three siblings and a brother-in-law in sudden and unexpected deaths is uncommon, I have also been faced with the tragic loss of friends through illnesses and even murder. Of course, as a member of the clergy, I have known the loss of many parishioners, most of whom were seniors and whose deaths were expected, but difficult nonetheless.

The good news is that we are not alone in our encounters of loss. Thankfully, our culture is waking up to the need to communicate our loss experiences. Communicating loss is essential. Communication is everything!

Unfortunately, not sharing my experience of my brother's suicide when I was in my early adolescence stunted my personal emotional growth. It triggered latent forms of depression and unhealthy activity even as I embraced a calling toward priestly life. Losing my sister and her husband through suicide when I was in the seminary should have prompted an expression of my feelings, but the fear of being labeled caused me to shut down my emotions, which resulted in additional depression in my early priesthood. The most recent loss of my younger sister by suicide in 2022 was met with a different, personal, healthier response. While I miss her terribly, I have acknowledged the need to express my feelings over this tragic death with numerous people and have addressed suicide, mental health, and grief head-on through the establishment of a full-time Office of Mental Health Ministry in the Diocese of Phoenix.

In our Office of Mental Health Ministry, we offer education for clergy, religious, and laypeople on mental disorders, grief, and general mental health care. We also advocate for additional studies in the mental health industry and enlist psychiatrists and counselors within the area as referrals for immediate and ongoing support. More importantly, the office provides multiple venues throughout the diocese for people to communicate their feelings of mental unrest, including grief—that universal experience that, left unattended, can cause deep and lasting harm.

Human beings must communicate. Communication is a God-given, built-in product of our brain that enables us to be happy, holy, psychosocially adept beings. With the aid of fMRI and other computer-age techniques, recent neurological studies show that communicating our feelings—hurts and joys—is necessary for connecting memories from the amygdala to the frontal lobe and other parts of the brain. Current studies insist that communication is as necessary as exercise, good eating, and adequate sleep to provide a sharper brain and a healthier mode of life.

For this reason, I am proud to offer this foreword in support of M. Donna MacLeod as she is offering an updated edition of the Seasons of Hope Catholic grief-support program. Building on the success of her previous publication, the Seasons of Hope *Leader's Guide* and accompanying *Journals* provide an excellent framework within which to communicate with others in person or online. COVID-19 brought the United States more than one million deaths as well as a rise in suicide, gun violence, addiction, homelessness, and social isolation. It is easy to feel alone in our world, and the death of one who is dear to us often multiplies our loneliness.

The methodology of Seasons of Hope includes opportunities for those who are struck with grief to join a parish group or online community at any time of the year. Each "season" of Seasons of Hope allows you to onboard and offboard at any time and with an invitation to return for a new season. Our own Office of Mental Health Ministry is adopting Seasons of Hope to keep the communication going. I am proud to say that this vehicle for connection may be found in hospitals, funeral homes, and parishes throughout our diocese.

Opportunities to communicate with others are essential. Opportunities to communicate with God are necessary. Seasons of Hope offers both types of opportunities, and as a bishop, I offer my wholehearted support and blessing.

Most Rev. John P. Dolan
Bishop of Phoenix

Introduction

Welcome to Seasons of Hope

Dear Grief-Support Colleagues,

Who among us can lose a loved one and remain the same? No one I know. The pain of mourning is a powerful catalyst. If my daughter Erynne had survived cancer in 1988, the Seasons of Hope ministry would not exist today. For years, my nursing career brought me to the dying and their families. What they taught me about grief, however, was insufficient. I had to walk the road of mourning myself to truly understand.

Although each grief journey is unique, kindred feelings flow among those of us who know devastating loss firsthand. When we entrust our grief-stricken selves to the Lord Jesus Christ, the healer of our souls, untold grace unfolds. We become a blessing to others who mourn. Some, like you and me, make it possible for his Church to reach out to the bereaved with a support group that truly consoles. Through four unique six-week seasons of Seasons of Hope each year, we link the bereaved with the Church, other parishioners of faith, and the Almighty in a most remarkable way.

Seasons of Hope is designed for easy adaptation in any parish, whether it's in the heart of a city or on a winding country road. Whether the brokenhearted from your faith community gather at the church or online for the sessions, they will be comforted. To help you get started, Part 1 of this *Leader's Guide* covers frequently asked questions:

- How do you assess the need for a Christ-centered grief-support group in your parish?
- What's the approval process in your parish?
- What does it take to organize Seasons of Hope?
- How do on-site and online sessions differ?
- What can you do to invite the bereaved?
- How does enrollment take place?
- What is faith sharing about?
- What do facilitators and helpers do?

- How does fellowship fit in?
- Is independent use of the *Journal* an option?

Here you will find helpful pointers about weekly on-site and online sessions to apply to the four seasons. This section also includes the basics about the *Journals*, the four companion booklets to the *Leader's Guide* that enhance both group sessions and personal growth through independent journaling at home. And it explores how the *Journals* can be used to comfort those who cannot participate in group sessions or perhaps prefer to attend to their grief on their own for whatever reason.

In part 2 of this book, you will find what we call "Footprints." Each Footprint, or session outline, serves as an easy-to-use script to lead a single group session. Each of the twenty-four sessions encourages participants with a lesson from Jesus about loss. Instead of focusing on a topic of grief as one might expect from many grief-support programs, each Seasons of Hope session explores mourning through scripture, prayer, reflection, activities, and faith sharing. This spiritually uplifting process opens broken hearts to the love of God, fostering a deeper appreciation of the Catholic Church.

The appendix has tools that make your preparation easier: a sample brochure, at-a-glance outlines of sessions and *Journals*, and a roster of suggested sound recordings and sacred images that can be useful during group or independent sessions. Want to deepen your understanding of grieving and its spiritual side? Check out the list of helpful team resources. In addition to books, it includes websites that provide information on professional and community support for losses that involve disenfranchised and/or complicated grief such as that experienced after suicide, overdose, murder, or child loss. Want some tried-and-true ministry leadership tips? This section also links you to avemariapress.com, the home of our Seasons of Hope facilitator-enrichment series of webinars and videos that builds upon the essential spiritual and practical advice of this *Leader's Guide*.

When parishioners ask why Seasons of Hope is offered, smile! Seasons of Hope parishes recognize Christ's call to console the bereaved. Through this ministry program, adults of all ages find Christ on their journey of sorrow. They have an opportunity to support each other and build up the faith community.

Whether your parishioners seek deeper meaning in their grief or simply need consolation, you will find that Seasons of Hope comforts through the Church's teachings and provides fresh ways to cope with sorrow. And for those in your group who are weary of feeling alone, it comforts beyond measure.

How grateful I am to God for the blessing of so many who made this updated edition of the Seasons of Hope *Leader's Guide* and *Journals* possible. Only God can make goodness flow from the sorrow we bear. And I truly believe the Seasons of Hope program embodied in these books is a powerful witness to that reality.

My heartfelt thanks remain with the clergy, family, friends, and bereaved who believed long ago that this work would enrich our parishes. They were right! I'm also grateful to everyone who lifts us up in prayer and to the brokenhearted who trust in the Lord and come to be comforted. I appreciate the priests, deacons, religious sisters and brothers, lay pastoral advisors, and diocesan leaders who welcome the program. And I admire the amazing Seasons of Hope facilitators and helpers, at my side and everywhere else, who have faithfully poured their gifts, talents, and compassion into season after season of this Catholic grief-support ministry. Their feedback is woven into this edition.

The ongoing enthusiasm and expertise of the Ave Maria Press professionals and staff are greatly appreciated. Many thanks especially to Eileen Ponder, Karey Circosta, Erin Pierce, and Stephanie Sibal for championing this updated edition.

As always, my husband Bryan's wisdom, love, faith, and generous spirit greatly influenced this work. I treasure the input of our dear daughter Meganne, who remains a constant source of love and support, and the memory of our dear Erynne, whose death opened my heart to all who mourn.

Jesus Christ embodies compassion. As you strive to imitate him in your ministry, may you discover his face among those who mourn. With Seasons of Hope groups, you can say to them with confidence, "Come and be comforted!"

In Christ our Hope,
M. Donna MacLeod

Part I

Bringing Seasons of Hope to Your Parish

Preamble

The Witness of Two Pastors

From the Church in Southern Oregon

When I came to Sacred Heart Catholic Church as pastor in 1998, M. Donna MacLeod made known to me her work with the bereaved in New England. Later, her desire—and mine—for a faith-based support group at our parish came to fruition with Seasons of Hope. By then Donna had chaired our pastoral council and coordinated our Disciples in Mission program, so I had ample evidence of her considerable talents as a planner, organizer, and motivator. As I expected, she put these skills to good use in expanding the New England version of Seasons of Hope and implementing the program in our parish.

What most drew me to Donna's vision for the program was its explicitly Catholic foundation. In contrast to secular support groups for the grieving, Seasons of Hope puts Jesus at the center and invites participants to entrust their loss and loneliness to him within the abundant, consoling wisdom of our Catholic tradition. Every session builds on a well-chosen passage from scripture and invites participants to share their loss experiences within the context of our faith, including devotion to the sacraments, Mary, and the saints.

Having just lost my mother, I was a natural candidate for participating in Seasons of Hope. Its well-structured format enhanced the efforts of those of us who became facilitators. When the sessions came to a close, I'd grown quite attached to my fellow group members and hated to see our time together end—as did all of us who took part. I hope the Lord will extend the consolation he brought us to all others who take up this work of renewal and peace.

Most Rev. Liam Cary
Bishop of Baker, Oregon
Former pastor of Sacred Heart Catholic Church
Medford, Oregon

From the Church in Massachusetts

I am most pleased to voice my support of the Seasons of Hope program. In a very busy parish community, I often struggle to know just how to follow through with parishioners after they have experienced significant life events such as baptisms, marriages, or funerals. Seasons of Hope pastorally addresses that need for those who have lost loved ones. Oftentimes, those who remain find themselves alone, sad, depressed, and perhaps angry. Seasons of Hope provides a community of support comprised of fellow parishioners who have experienced loss in their own lives. M. Donna MacLeod beautifully writes from her personal experience and her deep faith.

Many people in our community have become involved in Seasons of Hope. And one of the great aspects of this program is that, because it is framed into "seasons," there are opportunities throughout the year to invite grieving people to participate when they are ready to take that first step or return for some new group sessions.

Most important, Seasons of Hope engages the faith life of its participants and draws them into a deeper relationship with the living God, who "so loved the world that he gave his only Son, so that everyone who believes in him may not perish but may have eternal life" (Jn 3:16).

Seasons of Hope has brought hope, healing, peace, and love to so many who have participated in the program. It has been a profound blessing for our parish.

Rev. Msgr. Stephen J. Avila
Pastor of St. Joseph, Guardian of the Holy Family Parish
Falmouth, Massachusetts

One

The Decision

It's Personal

Choosing to offer a Christ-centered grief-support group for your parish is a decision that will change lives. The noble act of reaching out to the bereaved comes to us from Jesus, our Savior. He tells us in the Sermon on the Mount, "Blessed are those who mourn, for they will be comforted" (Mt 5:4). He decided that it would come to pass. We are simply his instruments. But what a privilege it is!

The call to minister to the grieving has already awakened within you; otherwise, this Seasons of Hope *Leader's Guide* would not have found its way into your hands. Bereavement outreach in the parish may currently be your life's work. Perhaps now is the time to offer a group or bring a fresh approach to meetings. Or maybe you're one of the first in your parish to recognize the need for a support group that gathers the bereaved together in Christ's name to share their faith, to find healing, and to be enriched by the consoling traditions of our Church—all worthy pursuits that stimulate the imagination. Think of all those who will benefit. What parish is spared dealing with death, dying, and funeral rites that may leave many feeling bereft? What about the deaths that parishioners encounter beyond the community of faith?

If you're like me, the death of a loved one broadsided you. Your pain is a powerful catalyst in Christ's hands; he heals your crushed spirit so that it soars again. You see clearly in your midst those who need consoling. The silence of their suffering touches your heart. Our hearts are lifelines to the Lord. The *Catechism of the Catholic Church* tells us: "The heart is our hidden center, beyond the grasp of our reason and of others; only the Spirit of God can fathom the human heart and know it fully. The heart is the place of decision" (2563). Trust it. Perhaps it is where we truly discern the voice of God.

St. Teresa of Calcutta had a discerning heart. Her life's calling to serve the suffering poor might never have been realized if she had not stooped down to pick up that first dying person on the street. She could have walked on by, for surely she was already engaged in worthy service to God, but she chose to help someone. She decided, and she acted on that decision. The face of Christ shone from those broken souls of Calcutta as surely as it radiates from our brothers and sisters who mourn. So, if you wonder whether one person can make a difference, just remember saintly Mother Teresa.

God also picks ordinary members of the clergy, religious, and laypeople to accomplish his goals. With Seasons of Hope groups, good people like you can bring Christ into the lonely suffering of the bereaved in our Church. Let's see how it's done.

It's about the Community of Christ

The parish is as complicated as any corporate bureaucracy when it comes to making decisions. You may be in a position to witness parish politics either make or break efforts to initiate new programs, or you may be outside that arena. I learned firsthand that timing is essential in parish life. Doors will open if you're in stride with God's time. Pray that you are.

Pray that your pastor, parish administrator (PA), or parish life coordinator (PLC) is too, because they are likely to be the ultimate decision-maker in the parish. Most pastors, PAs, and PLCs have heavy assignments and little time to spare. That doesn't mean yours won't be open to innovation. These leaders often deal with grieving families, and as people of compassion, they see that losing a loved one breaks many hearts and wounds many spirits. And if your parish leader has suffered through losing a dear one, this experience might color their response when you approach them about the need for a bereavement group.

Think positively. Whether you're a paid staff member or a volunteer with a calling, parish leaders usually respond positively to ideas that are well thought out, especially when an action plan is included. They must also perceive a need for a ministry. If you discover that your pastor, PA, or PLC has already decided a faith-sharing group for grieving parishioners is needed, thank God and skip to the next chapter!

Most of us have to do some legwork. Sometimes parish leaders want a fact-finding committee to weigh the pros and cons. Ask to be on it. Or you may be asked to investigate and report back. Whether you approach this alone, with a committee, or with the aid of funeral liturgy planners, be prepared to present a strong case.

The rest of this chapter will help you build that case. It uses questions that parish leaders and their advisors might pose while making a decision about Seasons of Hope. Your detective work connects you to staff and lay leaders you will work with in the future. Enjoy the encounters and know that the Lord is with you every step of the way!

Nine Factors to Assess before Making a Decision

1. How many parishioner deaths does your parish experience annually?

Research the last three years. A staff member is usually responsible for recording deaths for parish and diocesan records. The official book or computer file shows the name of the deceased, age, date of death, family contact or funeral director information, and other comments. The numbers give you a starting point. Then you can figure out if a widow, widower, or parents are left behind, but be aware that some potential participants (family members and friends) won't be obvious.

2. Is aging a significant element of your parish culture?

You probably have a good feel for the makeup of the parish simply by attending Masses scheduled at different times on the weekend. For hard statistics, check out a recent parish census that includes the homebound and residents of assisted-living facilities who can't attend Mass.

Chances are that a parish top-heavy with elders has more funerals per year than a community dominated by young families. Be inclusive in your thinking. One of my Seasons of Hope groups sprang from a task force studying the needs of seniors, but participants ranged in age from thirty-something on up.

3. What about deaths beyond the parish?

My experience shows that many who seek group support have lost a loved one from outside the parish. How do you get a handle on how many there might be? A helpful parish secretary is a godsend. If weekend Mass petitions include the names of deceased who are friends or family members of parishioners, the secretary probably gathered the information. The names may even be posted with those of deceased parishioners in the weekly bulletin or on the parish website.

Ask about requests for Mass intentions. If the Book of Remembrance is used in November, find out if it is popular. Parishioners who seek these forms of honoring their loved ones may be drawn to a group.

4. What is currently available in your parish?

It's good to talk with the staff or volunteers who help families prepare for a funeral. A parish may offer a variety of ministries that don't include a support-group experience for the bereaved. A Catholic women's group might help with an after-the-funeral gathering. A home-visit ministry may send condolence cards and reach out to widows and widowers.

Don't worry if a faith-sharing group for the grieving doesn't currently exist in your parish. Starting Seasons of Hope from scratch is the simplest path of all! A new program gets attention and draws volunteers interested in serving the bereaved. On the other hand, your parish may have a comprehensive consolation or grief-support ministry. Contact the coordinator to learn what services are in place. If a faith-sharing group is in the planning stage, your involvement may guarantee that Seasons of Hope happens.

What about those of you who currently run a support group as a staff member or volunteer? Do you use a secular format that emphasizes stages of grief and coping skills? Or perhaps your group has an open forum and social focus. These efforts are important, but many times a similar program is available in the wider community. Why not give parishioners a spiritual lift and a route to the Lord through their darkest hours?

Consider the benefits of Seasons of Hope:

- It's centered on Jesus Christ and grounded in the teachings of the Catholic Church.
- It explores mourning by using scripture, prayer, reflection, simple activities, and faith sharing.
- It gives the bereaved an opportunity to come together to share in God's love.
- It fosters healing and spiritual growth.
- It's a nurturing link to fellow parishioners of faith.
- The program's *Journals* encourage reflection on the scripture story after each small-group session and can be readily adapted for use by those working through the program independently.
- It provides four seasons consisting of six sessions each (twenty-four different themes), with flexibility for entering and leaving the program.

5. What about community resources?

Instead of offering a Catholic grief-support group, some parishes refer its members to local support groups. The grief-work model used by community-based organizations has merit and is suited for nondenominational settings. I ran such a program for hospice, so I can attest to its value. However, such offerings for the bereaved aren't meant to delve into matters of the soul. That responsibility truly lies with the parish.

6. Does a faith-based grief-support group fit the plans of the parish?

Every parish has some form of strategic plan for the future. Depending on the leadership style of parish leaders, the plan may exist in their minds alone, in the job descriptions of the staff, or in a formal document devised in concert with an advisory council that represents parishioners. Any way you look at it, a new offering like Seasons of Hope must fit the perceived needs of the parish and the timeline of current and upcoming projects.

In regard to future plans and parish events, the people in the know are the clergy, pastoral staff, and advisory councils (pastoral, administrative, and financial). If your parish communicates well with church members, plans may be posted on a bulletin board or website or published in a newsletter or weekly bulletin. It helps to review these sources before you contact the parish resource people.

To get an overview of scheduled parish events, investigate which meeting rooms are available in the months ahead. It may be premature to reserve space for Seasons of Hope, but take note of available slots that fit the six sessions per season. Each on-site session, including fellowship, takes about two hours. Add a little time for setup and cleanup.

Don't let limited room availability deter you. In a former parish, the only time the parish hall was available to us one season was on Sunday afternoons. Although it wasn't my team's first choice, we gave it a try. And it worked perfectly for retirees, those with full-time jobs, and the team. No one had to drive at night, and there was ample parking and access to on-site childcare. Today, scheduling online sessions eliminates any room-shortage issue. More guidance about meeting spaces can be found in the next chapter on page 18.

7. Who will do the work?

In Jesus's day, the harvest was plentiful, but the laborers were few (Mt 9:37). Things haven't changed much, have they? Be prepared for the show-stopping question: "Who is going to run this program?" Relax. It doesn't take an army. You want a facilitator to organize and lead the conversation at weekly sessions. Your best bet is a proven leader who can facilitate faith sharing and attract others to the ministry. The program can be successfully offered with volunteer lay leaders who have experienced loss of a loved one firsthand. My guess is you, or someone you know, will fit the bill. The rest is easy.

It takes only one facilitator (preferably with a "quiet" partner) for up to twelve participants. If a larger group is expected, have a backup facilitator on hand. Some parishes like to preregister or limit the number of participants to match the group size to the facilitators and the available space.

If your parish has faith-sharing groups that focus on evangelization or family life, experienced facilitators are in your midst. Some of them have lost a loved one and might like to assist with a Seasons of Hope group. Don't forget to recruit a few volunteers who just want to pitch in and help. No doubt their gifts and talents will come in handy.

It's also important to have an ordained or professionally trained lay ecclesial minister as a pastoral advisor for the program. (If one is also available as a teammate, rejoice!) Because of the spiritual nature of the sessions and the deep wounds of the bereaved, this is not the typical faith-sharing group that delves into the challenge of living in a secular world; rather, the sharing is deeply personal and soul baring. It is not a counseling session either, but a few kind words from a priest, deacon, or lay minister about God or the mystery of suffering can ease the burden the bereaved carry. Having the support and guidance of this spiritual advisor is also important for you as a program leader and mentor of ministry helpers.

8. What will Seasons of Hope cost each season?

A fiscally responsible parish looks at a program's price tag during the decision phase. So expect some questions. Here are basic items to consider:

- Books: Seasons of Hope *Leader's Guide* (one per teammate); Seasons of Hope *Journals* (one per participant and teammate each season)
- Publicity materials: brochures, bulletin inserts, posters, pastoral letter mailings
- On-site–specific items: name tags, markers, pencils, tissue boxes, prayer candle or other focal point, paper goods for refreshments
- Online-specific items: video communication license (if not already in place for the parish), booklet mailing

This bare-bones list works well for our team and keeps costs to a minimum. For on-site groups, it's simple to enhance the room with items from home or the parish (for example, a bell and a timer). We bring refreshments the first session and invite participants to pick a week to contribute a snack. If you aren't comfortable asking, include an estimate for snacks in the expense column.

On occasion, a pamphlet might be suggested for a session, but a cost-free alternative is given. Music is also optional. If participants don't have Bibles, the parish library or faith formation director might have some to lend. Any attempt to keep expenses down will benefit everyone involved.

If defraying costs is necessary to launch the program, each participant could pay for his or her *Journal* (or a portion of its cost). If the program is open to nonparishioners, charging them a fee is a reasonable option since they do not give financial support to the church.

In estimating costs, consider how many times a year to offer Seasons of Hope. You could do as many as four seasons a year. Each season is a distinct, stand-alone offering that fits the needs of new and returning members.

9. What benefits can you expect from Seasons of Hope?

Churchgoers will be happy that your parish offers Seasons of Hope. It tells them that church leaders, like you, have a finger on the pulse of parish life. Christ wants those who mourn to be comforted, and you give example by bringing him into their suffering. Expect the parish to be blessed because participants bond as Catholic people, building a strong sense of community that fosters stewardship.

Also consider how Seasons of Hope might benefit those who attend. If a neighboring parish offers the program, by all means talk to the people involved there. You will hear how fellowship with kindred souls helps lessen loneliness, a major concern after the loss of a loved one. Comfort also comes from the spiritual benefits of focusing on Christ.

Over the years, participants have completed surveys about the sessions they attended. Here's a representative sample of what we find time and again:

- "I learned some ways to bring more prayer into my grieving and remembering my loved ones. I also found some positive ways to help others and myself."

- "My time with Seasons of Hope has been so, so sweet and great! And the *Journal* helps me reach into my soul and write concerns that I had during my husband's dying."
- "Seasons of Hope lets me reflect on my grieving and be with the Lord."
- "It helps me to know that others want to talk about and remember their loved ones. I learned that the Lord does not leave us to grieve alone."

Don't be surprised if your team members discover blessings in their own lives. We did. My pastor in Medford, Oregon, wrote most eloquently about the benefits: "The best evidence I have for the value of Seasons of Hope is that none of us wanted it to end. Our Sunday afternoons together brought a compassionate appreciation for one another's struggles to let go of a loved one. We learned to let others into our struggle and to enter gently into theirs, to take strength and to give it. The program proved to be true to its name: we had helped each other to hope."

Presenting Your Assessments

Before you (and perhaps a fact-finding committee) present your findings to the pastoral staff (and possibly the advisory councils), it's best to organize your thoughts. I like to outline the major points and develop a handout for the meeting. You might use the questions listed under "Nine Factors to Assess before Making a Decision" as the headers for your findings. As with most committees, expect to submit a formal report that includes a recommendation.

It's easy to recommend Seasons of Hope. It works! Expect a question or two about the format. This *Leader's Guide* gives enough detail to boost your confidence. Plus you can share a Footprint of each session and one season's outlines (Sessions-at-a-Glance and *Journals*-at-a-Glance begin on page 160 in the appendix) to explain meetings and the home Soul Work feature. And check out the avemariapress.com/products/seasons-of-hope-facilitators-pack page for the facilitator-enrichment series that offers webinars and videos, which are packed with useful information on how to plan for and lead Seasons of Hope.

Christ is counting on you, so speak from the heart and present the facts. He will inspire your words. Then relax. When the decision comes to move forward, the next chapter ("First Steps") shows you where to begin.

Two

First Steps

How often do good ideas for your parish go undeveloped because no one knows quite where to start? You need clear vision to begin a faith-sharing group for the bereaved and the proper tools for the job. The Seasons of Hope *Leader's Guide* and *Journal* booklets provide the vision and proven means to accomplish a Christ-centered program that comforts those who mourn.

The rich diversity within the Church across America and beyond is awesome to behold. Each parish envisions Seasons of Hope through the lens of its unique history and culture, yet the steps to creating the program rely on common God-given gifts and talents of parish leaders. Whether you're a seasoned facilitator of a consolation ministry, a novice, or a supporter of the efforts, the following tips answer common questions about how to accomplish the mission.

Tasks of the Facilitator

(about eight weeks before sessions begin)

Where do you start?

When you undertake a ministry, look to the life of Jesus Christ for inspiration. Time and again, scripture shows that the Lord reverently prayed to the Father as he began and carried out his mission of salvation. The Seasons of Hope ministry is deeply rooted in prayer that seeks God's will. God wants to comfort those who mourn, and this program is an effective way to bring Christ to those who search for him in their grief.

As you prepare for this special outreach to mourners, consider ways that the parish can pray for the ministry. A powerful opportunity during Mass is the Universal Prayer, or Prayer of the Faithful. A petition could be added such as "For those who mourn in our parish—let our new Seasons of Hope group bring consolation." Check with the parish staff about how to go about this. If you attend daily Mass and can offer a petition from the pew, do so. Writing your request in the book of petitions also reaps the benefit of communal prayer. In addition, ask for prayer support from parishioners who serve the bereaved as funeral planners, as visitors to the homebound, or through prayer shawl or prayer partner ministries.

Meanwhile, continue to seek God's grace in your own prayer and know that others across the country are praying for you and your parish ministry. We ask God to pour out the Holy Spirit upon you so that you may be fully equipped to build his kingdom through acts of compassion for those who mourn.

What is the pastor's, parish administrator's, or parish life coordinator's role?

The Christ-centered nature of the program, with its use of scripture and Catholic traditions, makes it the perfect forum for a pastor, PA, or PLC to share personal knowledge and love of God with the brokenhearted. In the bereaved, we encounter the suffering face of Christ. When your parish leader believes that caring for those who mourn is as much a part of the Church's mission as administering the sacraments and spreading the Gospel, they will approve the formation of the Seasons of Hope ministry. How active your pastor, PA, or PLC becomes depends on that person's flexibility with scheduling and desire to personally reach those who mourn. To launch the program, the parish leader appoints a capable facilitator who understands the concerns of the bereaved. The ideal candidate is energetic, faith filled, organized, and creative, as well as a proven leader and a person of great compassion.

The facilitator could be a staff member who oversees family life, senior ministry, parish nursing, or spiritual aspects of the community or an interested volunteer who has leadership skills and firsthand knowledge of mourning. A volunteer leader would report to a pastoral advisor—either the pastor or a designated member of the pastoral staff. In this way, the Seasons of Hope ministry always receives pastoral guidance.

A pastor or pastoral staff member stirs up community interest in the preprogram phase each season. Whether attendance is encouraged through a homily, Mass announcements, a pastor's column on the website or in the bulletin, invitation letters, or by recommending Seasons of Hope to individuals in need, the wholehearted support of the pastoral staff sends a positive message to parishioners.

The pastor, PA, or PLC can also make a difference by welcoming participants at the beginning of each season or stopping by sessions to share words of encouragement, wisdom, and compassion. A group is specially blessed if such pastoral leaders offer a prayer, proclaim the Word, or answer questions of the faith that arise. This public and prayerful support from leadership strengthens the ministry.

What does it take to get Seasons of Hope rolling?

Ministering to the bereaved requires gifts, talents, and trust in the benevolence of God. If you are the facilitator, take a moment to give thanks. The Lord has called you, and that will bring you joy and peace.

As facilitator, you will

- organize the ministry,
- seek teammates,
- implement each season,
- and involve your pastoral advisor and teammates in decisions and tasks.

The list below is a guide to launching the first season. The timeline is just a guide. Feel free to add to it, omit some tasks, change the order, or revisit it to plan for next season.

Preparation Timeline

Facilitator Tasks

When	What
About eight to ten weeks before the first session begins	☐ Meet with pastoral advisor ☐ Determine target population ☐ Decide Seasons of Hope year ☐ Schedule chosen facility for the year ☐ Arrange Universal Prayer/Prayer of the Faithful intentions at weekend Masses ☐ Explore speaker campaign at weekend Masses ☐ Contact parish organizations to arrange a Seasons of Hope speaker ☐ Recruit ministry teammates ☐ Order team *Leader's Guides* and *Journals* ☐ Compile list of community resources

Team Tasks

When	What
About six weeks before the first session begins	☐ Plan promotion and needed teamwork ☐ Provide information to staff and clergy ☐ Create/display brochures

PART 1

	☐ Make/post promotional signs ☐ Submit all bulletin announcements ☐ Compile mailing list/mail invitations ☐ Investigate on-site childcare options ☐ Begin Universal Prayer/Prayer of the Faithful intentions at weekend Masses
Four weeks before	☐ Plan details of weekly sessions (see chapter 4) ☐ Discuss role of facilitator(s) (see chapter 3) ☐ Decide tasks at sessions ☐ Order Seasons of Hope *Journals* ☐ Continue Universal Prayer/Prayer of the Faithful intentions at weekend Masses
One to three weeks before	☐ Speak at organizations and weekend Masses ☐ Register participants by phone, email, or website ☐ Arrange for on-site refreshments and room setup ☐ Get Bibles for group use on-site ☐ Continue Universal Prayer/Prayer of the Faithful intentions at weekend Masses

The rest of this chapter addresses questions that arise during preseason planning, team building, promotion, and enrollment.

Mapping Out the Ministry

When should you meet with the pastoral advisor?

The earlier you share your vision for the year with your pastoral advisor, the better. Most of this section requires approval from parish leadership, so seek advice up front.

What about intentions during the Universal Prayer/Prayer of the Faithful?

Any Seasons of Hope activity that takes place at Mass needs pastoral approval.

What will the Seasons of Hope ministry offer this year?

It's best to schedule the year in advance. An active Seasons of Hope ministry will draw participants to all four seasons.

Is the order of seasons important?

No. Seasons are numbered one through four for ease of reference, not because one builds upon another. Each season welcomes newcomers and former participants with unique material.

Who should get a *Leader's Guide* and *Journal*?

The Seasons of Hope *Leader's Guide* is an essential tool for the ministry's decision-makers, promoters, and teammates. Provide the companion *Journal* booklets to round out everyone's understanding of the ministry. Group participants need the *Journal* for whichever season is going to be used. The *Journal* is used during group sessions and for home activities. For parishioners who cannot attend on-site or online sessions but would welcome support, many parishes provide a *Journal* for independent use and follow up with weekly phone calls from the team. Clarify with the pastoral advisor whether the booklets are a gift to parishioners (and possibly nonparishioners) or whether a donation to defray costs is expected. If donations are collected, discuss the cost per booklet and ask how to handle the proceeds.

How do you estimate how many will come?

Predicting is tricky business. Parish death records within the recent past may identify grieving families, but not everyone will want to join a bereavement group. You also need to think about those who lose someone beyond the parish. How can you reach them? You could estimate five to ten participants, the average size of a grief-support group. Some parishes choose the group size and register accordingly. Turnout, however, can exceed your wildest expectations even with preregistration, so order extra booklets.

Who will come to the group?

Seasons of Hope focuses on the spiritual side of grieving, so it appeals to those who are searching for Christ in the midst of their sorrow. When it is offered by a diocesan team, it welcomes participants from parishes throughout the region. But most Seasons of Hope groups are offered by Catholic churches for their bereft parishioners. In my experience, bereaved Christians of other denominations who come to our groups also find the program quite helpful.

When a group is limited in size because of available facilitators or seating, who attends can become an issue. Do you reserve openings solely for parishioners? Decide beforehand with your pastoral advisor.

PART 1

Should you investigate childcare options?

Yes, if the parish has a significant percentage of young bereft families, childcare assistance during group sessions could help parents attend. Find out whether there are trained/certified staff or volunteers and a parish room that is equipped for childcare available for non-Mass hours. If so, will the parish cover the expense? The care provider would need to make plans, and you'd need to book the playroom and include childcare in promotional materials. Seek a six-week commitment, but make the provider aware that the service depends on enrollment.

What is the best time frame in which to offer sessions?

The Seasons of Hope design has the group meet for six consecutive weeks (or one season) at a time. It takes commitment to come each week, but commitment creates trust among participants and a positive atmosphere for faith sharing. Four unique seasons are available. A break of at least four weeks between seasons is recommended. This gives the team a chance to reboot, recruit, and then welcome newcomers and returning or ongoing participants. Forming a new group and providing a new season of material for the journey encourages growth of the ministry and keeps it vibrant and welcoming.

Where do you hold sessions?

If at all possible, keep the same setting and schedule for the season. Parish facilities work nicely for Seasons of Hope groups of all sizes. The site gives a clear message that the Church cares about its bereaved. A parish hall is convenient and usually can be easily accessed by everyone, including those using a walker or wheelchair. Chairs and parking are plentiful, and kitchen facilities and sometimes childcare are available too. If you book a room at the parish, add time before and after the two-hour session for setup and cleanup.

If a parish facility is unavailable, online sessions are worth pursuing. (See chapter 5.) A home setting that's not far from the church could also be considered. The group size would be limited by ease of access, seating capacity, and parking. An alternate site and a plan to notify participants would be needed in case the homeowner becomes ill or has an emergency.

What makes a good meeting room?

Select a room that fits the size of your anticipated group and has space to mingle during fellowship. The room should provide privacy, adequate lighting, climate control, and electric outlets for music players and coffee and tea makers. Also consider whether noise from outside the room will pose a problem.

What time is best for on-site sessions?

Each parish selects a time for its sessions based on the availability of the team and site. Ask your advisor about parish events that may affect promotion or attendance. The time and setting you select will influence who comes. The employed may prefer online groups or on-site sessions in late afternoons, in evenings, or on weekends. Those who don't drive after dark prefer on-site daytime sessions or online evening offerings. If possible, pick a day and time that makes a visit by the clergy or lay pastoral advisor feasible.

What about ministry expenses?

Seasons of Hope is a low-budget ministry, but expenses do come up. The advisor may have you contact the parish business manager to submit receipts for reimbursement. If considering online groups, see if a video communication license exists for the parish and whether it can be used by this ministry or would be reimbursed. Also discuss whether brochures and signs should be copied on office machinery or sent out for printing.

What other advice might a facilitator need?

See if the parish nurse, leaders of social service ministries, or a nearby Seasons of Hope facilitator has a list of local grief counselors and special-need survivor groups to share. If not, compile a list in the event that someone asks about community options. The appendix section "Helpful Resources for the Team" has information on national programs that can connect you to local chapters and counselors.

If you plan to recruit volunteers to help with the ministry, talk with the pastoral advisor about your choices or ask for names of possible candidates. Once you meet with the advisor, you can set the ministry wheels in motion.

Building a Team

How do you recruit Seasons of Hope helpers?

Jesus could have conducted his ministry on his own, but he chose to surround himself with helpers. You don't have to undertake a ministry alone either. Although Seasons of Hope doesn't require a crowd of consolation ministers to accomplish its goal, having a companion or two on the journey blesses your efforts.

Opportunities to serve go beyond running sessions and facilitating faith sharing. Some prefer to help with preseason planning, publicity, and mailings. During the season, some are greeters, registrars, or readers of the Word, while others are involved with refreshments, setup, or cleanup. The trick to building a compatible team is to welcome all who want to serve, find something that interests them, and then let them do it.

Recruitment can begin with a bulletin announcement. When you invite the community to help with Seasons of Hope, you spread the word about it. It's a perfect way to reach newcomers and parishioners who want to serve the bereaved.

[Sample Recruitment Announcement with Seasons of Hope Logo]

Seasons of Hope Catholic Grief Support Is Coming in June!
Volunteers Needed.

A unique Christ-centered faith-sharing group for the bereaved will be offered at Sacred Heart on six Mondays this summer. The facilitator is looking for some helpers with this new ministry. It's not a huge time commitment, but your effort will help many. Please contact Mary Davis at 555-XXX-XXXX for ways to get involved.

Another good starting point is people you know in the parish. Prayerfully reflect on those who have adjusted well to losing a loved one. Rejoice if someone comes to mind who has a strong faith in God, has compassion and patience with others, listens well, keeps confidences, works well with you and others, and is available to serve. Such a person is a gift from God, so make that call!

You can seek input from parish staff, leaders of related ministries, or council members who represent the parish at large. The parish computer database may also have the names of parishioners who indicate experience with consolation ministry. Don't forget to invite a parish priest, deacon, or lay pastoral staff member with a recent loss or chaplaincy experience.

Once Seasons of Hope is underway, a new source of volunteers will exist in former participants. They know the benefits and may feel called to minister to others.

What's the best way to contact unknown candidates for the team?

Consider whether the culture of your parish tends to be formal. If so, send a letter of introduction or an email before making blind calls to candidates you don't know. Here's an example:

[Sample Invitation to Potential Team Member]

SACRED HEART CATHOLIC CHURCH

1234 Main Street • Anytown, USA
Phone: 123-4567 • Rectory: 123-4567

Dear______________,

Sacred Heart needs people of compassion to offer a Seasons of Hope faith-sharing group to those who mourn. Leaders in the parish tell me that you have gifts and talents that could help the ministry make a difference. This summer, six sessions are planned for Mondays from June 11 through July 16.

A brochure is included. Perhaps you would like to get involved. I will call in a week to discuss the details with you. Meanwhile, please keep Seasons of Hope in your prayers as you consider serving those in need of consolation.

Sincerely,
Mary Davis
Facilitator, Seasons of Hope
555-XXX-XXXX

Are phone calls a good approach?

Calling potential volunteers without a prior letter or email works nicely in some parishes. Let the person know that you represent the parish and how you received their name, and say you are recruiting for the ministry.

Some want to hear about Seasons of Hope right then or may ask to meet with you. Some want information emailed to them. Others like time to think about the request. Any of those responses gives the person an opportunity to discover how prepared and flexible you are. You also get a sense of their interest.

Expect to get at least one "No, thank you" during the search. Direct, decisive people know their limits and don't waste time. What a blessing for you! You don't need someone who will back out at the last minute. But before you let the person off the hook, find out if they know of a potential volunteer. The response might be the lead you're looking for.

PART 1

What's the next step?

When one or more of those you contact express interest in the ministry, set up a meeting. I like to send a follow-up note by mail or email.

[Sample "Welcome to the Team" Letter]

SACRED HEART CATHOLIC CHURCH

1234 Main Street • Anytown, USA
Phone: 123-4567 • Rectory: 123-4567

Dear________________,

I am delighted you will join in our efforts at Sacred Heart to comfort those who mourn. As we discussed, the program planning meeting is on Sunday, April 22, at 3:00 p.m. in the Parish Center. If you have any questions, feel free to call me at 555-XXX-XXXX.

Meanwhile, please keep Seasons of Hope and those we serve in your prayers.

In Christ our Hope,
Mary Davis
Facilitator, Seasons of Hope

What happens at the prospective volunteer meeting?

Whether it's done one-on-one over a cup of coffee or with a group, share the Christ-centered approach of Seasons of Hope and what participants will gain. Use this chapter and the checklist in chapter 4 (p. 53) to explain what the team does, or show the introductory video from the Seasons of Hope facilitator-enrichment series at www.avemariapress.com. Before you finish, confirm each person's desire to serve.

What makes a good Seasons of Hope team?

Find a way to involve each volunteer, and your team will thrive. Make praying together before each session a priority. Give thanks to God for each other and for the brokenhearted ones who come. Working together for the Lord brings joy to the ministry.

Promoting the Program: Team Tasks

(about six weeks before sessions begin)

How do you get the word out?

Promotion is an important step to bring Christ to those who mourn. Know the gifts and talents of your team and involve them in getting the word out.

What about a Seasons of Hope logo?

The Seasons of Hope logo can be downloaded from www.avemariapress.com/products/seasons-of-hope-facilitators-pack/ to use on items that promote the program. Be sure items marked with the logo cite "Used with permission" and "All rights reserved."

What about a brochure?

A Seasons of Hope brochure (from a double-sided 8.5" × 11" sheet) can be specific to a season or created for year-round use. Each column or panel has a job. The first side has a title, reasons why people come to the ministry, and a blank middle panel (the back) for parish-specific information and the Seasons of Hope copyright notice. The second side has the program overview, registration information, and a column for insights from participants. See the appendix for a sample (p. 158) and visit www.avemariapress.com/products/seasons-of-hope-facilitator-pack/ for a template to create your own customized brochure.

Whether you use the sample text in the appendix or create your own, try different fonts, paper weights, and colors to find what best suits your offering. Add the Seasons of Hope logo and your church logo to the front panel if you like. Parchment stationery folds the best for brochures; however, it costs a little more than copier paper.

Strategically place your brochures. A clear, upright stand with space for a poster and brochures gets noticed on an information table. Think beyond the racks in the church, parish hall, and office. Brochures work best when they are coupled with a letter, a speaker campaign, or one-on-one contact.

Who else gets a brochure?

Start with the parish secretary, staff, teammates, and clergy, both active and retired. Also be sure to include the parish pastoral council and perhaps the finance council. If possible, present the brochure at pastoral staff and council meetings to answer questions and seek referrals.

If home visitors or a parish funeral planner works with the bereaved, seek their support and give them a supply of brochures. Funeral home directors can also provide Seasons of Hope brochures to bereaved family members.

What about bulletin, newsletter, and website announcements?

Parish announcements can be an effective tool for reaching grieving members of the community, either directly or through friends. Find out the deadline and guidelines for submissions and whether email submissions are accepted. Aim to have announcements go out during the month before your group starts so that people can enroll. We email three announcements with different headings, the logo, and dates well in advance of the office deadline for submissions.

[Sample Bulletin Announcement with Seasons of Hope Logo]

Seasons of Hope Group for the Bereaved Begins Soon!

If you're in need of consolation after losing a loved one, this Christ-centered faith-sharing group is for you. It meets for six Mondays beginning June 11. Prayer, scripture, faith sharing, and fellowship begin at 10:00 a.m. For more details, take a Seasons of Hope brochure at the church entrance or call Mary Davis, 555-XXX-XXXX.

What about bulletin board announcements?

Check with the office staff about posting announcements on bulletin boards. Some parishes assign space to each ministry. A good location to promote Seasons of Hope is any place where parishioners can pause to read the flyer or poster. The best design is simple yet catchy. Choose a prominent phrase and a concise message. For example:

[Sample Flyer with Seasons of Hope Logo]

Seasons of Hope

Come and Be Comforted!

SEASONS of HOPE
A faith-sharing group for the bereaved begins
June 11 at 10:00 a.m. at the Parish Center.
Please take a brochure for details and sign up soon!

You don't have to be an artist or a computer whiz to make a flyer or poster, but why not ask someone with talent to donate what you need? A parish school often has a computer lab and an art teacher with students who do things for the church. Decide the number of flyers or posters needed and provide the Seasons of Hope logo, color preferences, lettering style, and design. An 8.5" × 11" size works well because it fits on most bulletin boards. Poster board or laminated paper holds up the best.

In addition to posting promotional signs at church entrances, include the parish office and hall, restrooms, and the chapel entry, and ask about posting in the school reception area, if available. Have extra signs to replace those that go home with parishioners. If the group meets at a parish facility, also make some "Welcome to Seasons of Hope" signs for the day of the program.

How about a letter to introduce the bereaved to the program?

A pastoral letter to all recently bereaved families in the parish is a powerful way to draw participants. The pastor may want to write the letter or approve a template you provide. You can verify when letters are delivered by mailing one to your own address. Feel free to adapt the following example to meet the needs of your parish.

[Sample Letter to the Bereaved]

Sacred Heart Catholic Church

1234 Main Street • Anytown, USA
Phone: 123-4567 • Rectory: 123-4567

Dear __________,

We/I extend to you our deepest sympathies for the loss of your __________.

As you know, mourning the loss of someone you love is never easy, but there is hope. Our Sacred Heart parish community will host Seasons of Hope, a unique support group for the bereaved. This program, rooted in Catholic tradition, conveys God's consolation through scripture, prayer, reflection, and sharing our faith.

I hope you and your family will read the enclosed brochure for details and prayerfully consider our/my invitation to come. The group meets at the Parish Center for two hours each Monday morning for six weeks beginning June 11. To save your spot, please call (name) at 555-XXX-XXXX or email at __________ by May 28.

Be uplifted, knowing that the Lord blesses those who mourn. Surely, Seasons of Hope is a way to find him in our midst.

Peace in the Lord,
Fr. Larry Deagon
Pastor, Sacred Heart Catholic Church

Mary Davis
Facilitator, Seasons of Hope

Some participants who received a similar letter told me that the personal nature of the invitation encouraged them to come. A form letter would have been a turnoff.

Where do you get a mailing list?

The team usually compiles the mailing list. When parish death records have family information, the job is easy. Decide which months the list will cover (usually six to twelve) and copy the information. When death records omit contact information for relatives, the team plays detective. You can contact the parish's funeral liturgy planner and then match names to a church directory, database, or telephone book.

Check your list with a longtime parishioner or a ministry leader who makes home visits. Such a person often knows the deceased and family. Get the pastor's, PA's, or PLC's input on the list, too. They know their flocks.

How about a speaking campaign?

Presenting Seasons of Hope to the community bolsters participation. Early on, contact organizations and ministries that serve the bereaved and ask to be on the next agenda. A five-minute presentation works. Provide brochures and use one to highlight key points. Then take questions from the audience. Some who are present may need the support group, so invite them to come. Ask everyone to be ambassadors for Seasons of Hope and to pray for those who mourn.

Which church groups do you approach?

The pastoral council, women's and men's organizations, couples' clubs, seniors' groups, prayer groups, adult formation groups, Bible studies, parent meetings for children in religious education and the parish school if there is one, as well as sacramental preparation programs, including RCIA teams, are all potential audiences for fruitful speaking engagements. Other opportunities may exist in your parish. If a speaking opportunity can't be arranged, provide Seasons of Hope brochures for the various group leaders to distribute at meetings or send via email. Most will be happy to oblige.

What about presentations at weekend Masses?

A pre-Mass announcement included with other parish news helps to spread the word. It's even more effective if your priest talks about Seasons of Hope from the pulpit. And some pastors welcome ministry speakers. If so, get approval early so the presentation is given at least two weekends before the season begins. A three-minute talk is the norm, and one written from the heart is more powerful than rattling off dates and times. The speaker should be certain to arrive in plenty of time before each Mass, check in with the sacristan and priest celebrant, and practice with the church microphone beforehand. Decide whether to host a registration table after Masses.

What about a church website?

Most parishes have a website that offers bulletin information or a parish calendar of events. This is a good way to advertise Seasons of Hope. It also helps to post a short announcement of the upcoming sessions and a pdf of the Seasons of Hope brochure to provide details. The website could also have a portal for those who want to contact the team to enroll.

How do you reach the bereaved who don't attend Mass regularly?

Some find it difficult to return to church after the funeral Mass of a loved one. Maybe the surroundings bring back sad memories, or the one who mourns feels anger toward God. In such circumstances, the concern of a relative or friend might be needed to draw the bereaved in. During promotion, encourage parishioners to take a Seasons of Hope brochure to share with those who are not attending Mass. Some parishes reach nonpracticing members through the local newspaper's community events page.

Responding to Prospective Participants

How do you handle inquiry calls?

Bereaved callers often have details of Seasons of Hope in hand. Most, in my experience, call to determine if the group is right for them.

What can you do? Be you. Find out why the person called. Listen with genuine interest as the story unfolds. Offer a kind word or two. Answer any questions. Compassion shows the essence of a group experience better than a sales pitch.

When it's clear the caller wants to enroll, use a form to record contact information. We use a form that includes space to check off a few items that help us better understand the person's loss and desire for a faith-based group.

[Sample Form to Enroll Participants]

Seasons of Hope Season ____________ On-site___ Online ___

Name ______________________________________ Phone ________________________

Street or post office box ____

Apt. # _________________

City ____ Zip code _________________

Email ____

Goes to _____________ Church

Learned about Seasons of Hope from ____

Name of deceased and relation ____

Date of funeral ____

Anticipated loss? _______________________ Sudden loss? _______________________

Attended a support group? ____

Caller shared he/she is ____

Special physical needs? ____

Home Bible? _______________________________ Zoom access? __________________

Date of call and/or sign-up ____

Confirmed by email on ____

If our program doesn't fit the parishioner's schedule, we share when our next season will begin and also suggest that the current *Journal* can be used independently with a weekly support call from the team. Other Seasons of Hope offerings in nearby parishes or community-based support may also be options for the caller to consider.

How do you respond to those who contact you through the website?

You would arrange to speak with the person about their loss and their questions, and record the findings on the usual enrollment form.

What obstacles do some of the bereaved face when they need support?

When grief involves a loss that many in society have difficulty acknowledging, such as suicide, overdose, murder, or the death of an infant, the bereaved may fear others will dismiss their pain or harshly judge them or their departed loved one. With sudden or other traumatic loss, many fear that no one can relate to their pain except people who have the same type of loss. Some find their way to a special survivor group or professional counseling to work through their issues with their loved one's circumstances. That is a very positive step toward healing.

What if an inquirer's grief needs special attention?

We strive to meet the bereaved where they are. Some are looking for a special survivor group or the names of grief counselors. We use our list of local resources and let them know Seasons of Hope is there for them, too, if they'd like to focus on the spiritual side of grieving.

Some will call after they've benefited from clergy support, a survivor group, or one-on-one grief counseling. They tend to blend well into Seasons of Hope groups because they are ready to rely on their faith and seek the consolation only God can give.

Sometimes people who enroll don't let on that their loss involves a complex, troubling situation. Yet you may suspect something is amiss that's beyond the continuum of so-called normal grieving. In that situation, I make sure the person partners up with a teammate for the first session's one-on-one activity. That's when details of loss are first addressed in the group. The participant gets an attentive listener and needed support, and we gain a deeper sense of the state of the person's grieving.

Whatever response we have to the needs of those who come, it helps to keep sight of our mission for Christ. He is the consoler and healer. We are simply caring companions who walk beside his beloved bereaved.

For information and links to sites on grief in general and special situations that many parishioners face, check out Helpful Resources for the Team in this *Leader's Guide* appendix.

Are new participants added throughout the season?

No. We recommend that any promotion item include the date when enrollment ends, which ideally is a few days before the sessions begin. That way the team can properly prepare for those who reserved a spot. If someone can only start in the second session, we go over the first session's program details during the enrollment call. Week two is the last entry point. Anyone who calls after that will have missed too much of the program, so we share information on our future offerings and other resources in the wider community.

How do you handle walk-ins?

We suggest having a couple of extra *Journals* and enrollment forms at the welcome table for the first session. The greeter would have the person meet with a facilitator, preferably before the session begins, to enroll them and provide the booklet.

What is the mix of participants in the average Seasons of Hope group?

Expect your recruitment efforts to draw substantially more women than men. Pictures from my groups around the country testify to that. Most Seasons of Hope groups have a mix of bereft spouses; parents who have lost an infant, child, teen, or adult child; and other adults who mourn the death of parents, siblings, or friends. But a parish with many bereft young families may group those couples together. Or a parish in a retirement area may have groups that are mostly widows and widowers. The losses that bring participants together vary, but their heartfelt desire for the consolation only God can give is what makes Seasons of Hope groups special.

What's next?

You now have some tools and the basics on how to structure Seasons of Hope, recruit helpers, rally support in the faith community, enroll participants, and refer those who need further grief support. The next chapter, "Faith Sharing, Facilitators, and Fellowship," focuses on the dynamics of faith sharing and your role as a facilitator of Seasons of Hope sessions.

Three

Faith Sharing, Facilitators, and Fellowship

For some of us, losing a loved one is a devastating experience that can change the way we look at life. The intensity of our grief and how long mourning will linger often depend on how close we were to the deceased, the history of that bond, and other losses we have suffered in the past.

Grief brings pain whether it is expressed through emotions, physical symptoms, or disturbing behaviors that prompt us to seek help. When we are people of faith, we may sense that our spirit is wounded as well. Although the consolation of Christ surrounds us during bereavement, the throes of grief can blind us to it.

This chapter lays the cornerstone for a Christ-centered Seasons of Hope group in your parish. It offers new and veteran consolation ministers plenty of ideas about the essence of faith sharing, effective facilitating, and the healing power of fellowship.

The Essence of Faith Sharing

Did Jesus leave us any clues on faith sharing?

Faith sharing is not something new. The final chapter of the Gospel of Luke gives us a glimpse of how Jesus shared the faith with his bereaved disciples. He appeared to two of them on the road to Emmaus while they were discussing his death and debating what had happened.

Even though the pair did not recognize their Savior, Jesus asked a question that enabled them to pour out their grief. It seems he listened attentively to their expressions of sorrow and hope. Then he brought the scriptures to life to strengthen their faith in him. The framework for bereavement faith sharing was born.

Who seeks a bereavement faith-sharing group?

The simple answer is the bereaved among us who practice the faith and look to the Church for support during mourning. Some may have read numerous self-help books about loss. Some have sought counseling. Others have attended a support group that emphasizes stages of grief and coping skills. Others have been drawn to a group that focuses on their specific type of loss. Such groups are a great help with day-to-day matters or sensitive issues related to a loved one's death, but many do not delve deeply into spiritual concerns or the journey of faith. For those who hunger for God's consolation from within the tradition of the Catholic Church, Seasons of Hope can nourish the soul.

Those of us who look to God for guidance tend to recognize signs of the divine in the world and in everyday life. Church may be the only place where we meet others who willingly acknowledge God's presence. Even in a parish setting, however, finding those who are comfortable sharing their faith can be a challenge.

When we come to a Seasons of Hope session, we are much like the disciples on the road to Emmaus. We, too, are people of faith who feel a need to talk about a deceased loved one. We may feel confused by our loss. Sorrow and hope drift through our thoughts. Like the Emmaus disciples, we may not recognize Christ in our midst or relate our trials of mourning to his suffering. Yet we want help. Seasons of Hope uses scripture stories and faith-sharing questions based on these stories to point us to the Lord, our consoler.

What exactly is faith sharing in relation to mourning?

Faith sharing is a process that lets us view mourning through the lens of scripture. It helps us explore our losses and belief in God by relating to Jesus and others in the Bible. In so doing, we open ourselves to Christ's consolation and healing. The process encourages us to be comforted in the Lord and to acknowledge, affirm, and appreciate the suffering and victories of others in the group.

What is appropriate group etiquette for faith sharing?

A facilitator guides the process by keeping the focus on the questions and the Lord. A facilitator doesn't teach, preach, or advise, and neither should anyone else in the group. The facilitator creates a safe place for participants to express their feelings about loss and receive consolation. Participants are asked to commit to a simple code that demonstrates respect for the group and its individual members.

Group members agree to

- come each week and make it known if they can't;
- arrive on time;
- treat others with respect;
- share their faith story and then let others talk;

- be a good listener;
- keep what is shared in confidence; and
- be open to God touching them through others.

Effective Facilitators

Is the facilitator an advisor?

No, although it's tempting to give advice when asked. As a facilitator, you can certainly share your experience with loss. That builds trust. But whatever eased your pain and grief may not be helpful for everyone. Through the faith-sharing process you hope participants listen to the promptings of their own heart and soul. That is where God places his answers.

What is the facilitator's role during faith sharing?

Faith sharing works best if one facilitator poses the session's questions to the group and guides the conversation when needed. A cofacilitator or helper, who may be a facilitator trainee, serves as a "quiet" partner.

The quiet partner sits on the opposite side of the circle and surveys group dynamics. This teammate signals the facilitator if anyone gets overlooked during the sharing, so that all are included. The partner adds their own story during faith sharing, monitors the time, and serves as a backup facilitator if an additional group is needed.

After the session, the facilitator and partner take time to review and evaluate in a supportive way their efforts during the group. They discuss what transpired and assess the process. They might want to switch roles for a session or two during a season. Most groups adjust easily, and quietly observing the group process can sharpen one's skill as a facilitator.

How many facilitators are needed for a group session?

Whether your group is large or small, one facilitator is all that is needed to preside during the Opening, Activity, and Summary. It's wise to have an additional facilitator and quiet partner for the faith-sharing segment when there are twelve or more participants. Subgroups provide more time for responding to the questions and can be formed according to types of losses, if desired.

Does a facilitator need a counseling degree?

No. Seasons of Hope is not professional counseling. It is lay ministry. Experience with small groups or a faith-sharing group is desirable, though. If you're a person of hospitality and compassion, you will likely facilitate well. Your skill at speaking and listening as well as your experience with bereavement come into play as you encourage the group to journey together.

How can you prepare to be an effective facilitator?

One of the best resources to refer to is the book of your life—your own experience with loss, grief, and communicating with God and others. To build confidence, you can study works on group leading, grief theory, and mourning (see resources in the appendix). Or you might attend any consolation ministry training provided by your diocese or another local Catholic organization. You can also observe a facilitator who makes the process look easy or spend time with a mentor. Do more if you like, but be gentle with yourself. Experience as a facilitator is the greatest teacher of all.

Is there a spiritual dimension to facilitating?

Yes. Pray that God gives you what you need to do his will and stay open to the brokenhearted people he sends you. Then trust. When I guide a group, I usually don't recall catchy phrases the experts find helpful in a pinch. I respond from the core of my being, from the sympathetic heart that God has given me. When you respect yourself and the participants in the circle, you allow the Holy Spirit to bring out the best in each of you.

How does the charism of hospitality fit in with facilitating?

As a facilitator, you invite participants to share their stories of loss with the group, and like Jesus on the road to Emmaus, you listen attentively.

What does attentive listening involve?

It means paying attention to the facts of the participant's story and the emotions expressed. Even when someone doesn't name feelings, body language often gives a hint. For example, are the person's shoulders squared, hands clenched, and eyes closed as he or she speak? What words do the participant use in sharing their story? Shocked? Sad? Angry? Guilty? Lonely? Overwhelmed? Relieved? At peace? What do their words tell you? When you're not sure, verify your perception by briefly reflecting back to that individual what you see and hear.

Your body language is also important. Facing the person and maintaining eye contact communicate interest and encourage sharing. Uncrossed arms and legs convey an attitude of openness to the speaker. Responding in a supportive manner to each participant fosters an atmosphere of acceptance. In such a climate, the group learns to trust the process.

What are some tips for posing faith-sharing questions?

You want to guide the process without dominating it. Some facilitators like to give an example from their own loss to initiate sharing. Sometimes that's necessary, but those comments usually influence what participants say. Instead, start by posing a question from the Footprint and let participants go where they need to go with it.

Your goal isn't to teach, give a sermon, or talk a lot about yourself. But it is appropriate to witness to your own loss and to acknowledge, affirm, and appreciate others. Your efforts make sharing easy and enjoyable for them.

What's the best way to handle silence?

Don't fret when silence reigns. Many participants need time to think before they speak, so resist the urge to fill the quiet. If the pause makes the group uncomfortable, repeat or rephrase the question or move on to another. If silence seems to have nothing to do with the question, get feedback on what is happening in the group. It may be as simple as everyone being distracted by noise nearby or the arrival of a stranger.

Sometimes participants aren't comfortable sharing with the group, yet they return each week. Maybe their loss was recent and they are afraid that speaking will intensify their grief. With time, they usually open up. Others may be shy or simply reserved. They might benefit from some gentle coaxing. If such a person is nodding yes as another speaks, I might say to her, "You look like you can relate to that . . . "

Sometimes silent participants want to remain anonymous. Perhaps their loss involves suicide, overdose, homicide, abortion, a dreaded disease, or scandal. Or they harbor deep-rooted ill feelings toward the deceased that they dare not share. If that kind of situation is revealed during faith sharing, it demands great sensitivity. The facilitator and any team members present must respond as compassionately as they would with any other deep-felt revelation, lending visible support without prying or taking on the role of a counselor. You would want to talk with the participant outside the group, possibly to share information on additional support, such as a survivor support group or grief therapist.

How does a facilitator maximize sharing?

Each faith-sharing group has a personality all its own. As in any healthy relationship, participants become more comfortable with each other as time passes. You deal with several factors when you pose a question to the group. Initially, you respond to the individual who replies first, and then you ease others into sharing. After a few sessions, a healthy group needs less prompting from you to share with one another.

As you and the group listen to a faith story, whether it is heart-wrenching or uplifting, the one speaking receives attention and a message of affirmation and acceptance from the group. Participants are receptive to questions when they sense that what they say will be valued. You can thank them for sharing with words, smiles, nods, or other gestures. Acknowledging and appreciating each participant encourages participants to affirm each other.

How do you handle emotional reactions in the group?

Some bereaved never join a group because speaking about their loss brings an emotional meltdown. Those who find the courage to attend have similar concerns. No matter how clearly you explain that the group is a safe place to let tears and emotions flow, participants struggle to control their grief reactions. When participants cry and their words get choked off, don't panic. And don't automatically pass a box of tissues to them unless they look for one. An unsought tissue is often interpreted as a signal to stop crying. Crying actually releases emotions, helping the person.

When someone can't go on talking, you can respect his or her grieving with quiet attention. If it feels right, offer a petition that lifts the person up to the Lord. Use whatever comes to you at the moment. I might say,

> Lord, our friend Laurie is filled with sorrow right now.
> We lift her broken heart up to you. Bring peace to her.
> We ask in your name. Amen.

When "Laurie" has taken a deep breath and looks at you, you might concisely repeat her story before the meltdown to validate it with her and encourage her to go on. Whether her decision is to continue with the tale or decline, she discovers acceptance. Often the sad moment is a great gift, because other participants generally speak up and relate to the person's grief.

What if a participant has spiritual distress?

For some, the spiritual wounds of losing a loved one are so deep that the person experiences troubling faith-related shame, guilt, abandonment, hopelessness, or anger. Those in spiritual distress may not be able to speak openly about their relationship with God, relate their grieving to the session scripture stories, or attempt to relate to the faith stories of others. They may be uninterested in the sacraments and consoling traditions of the Church. If you think it could help, by all means discuss with the person the idea of speaking to a priest or other pastoral staff member who can give them more assistance. If in doubt, ask for input from your pastoral advisor and proceed accordingly.

If someone's distress, however, involves despair or thoughts of self-harm, promptly seek assistance from your pastoral advisor.

As a facilitator, how do you set the pace for sharing?

It comes as a surprise to some participants when the mood of sharing is upbeat. Sharing the joy our deceased loved ones once brought is just as welcome during faith sharing as tears. No matter what the mood of the session, aim to finish the faith-sharing segment on time. Have your partner signal when ten and five minutes remain. If everyone in the group hasn't spoken yet, you will still have time to draw in the quiet ones.

What is the best way to keep the focus on Christ?

When a participant or the group wanders away from the posed question, a simple "We' re getting off track. The question is . . . " usually does the trick.

How do you handle someone who starts to ramble?

Sometimes a participant pours out a story that seems endless. People start to fidget. What do you do? Wait for the speaker to take a breath and then interrupt? Perhaps, but try to do it in a respectful way. Think about the examples Jesus gave us.

Would he listen carefully? Would he reflect back the pain, sorrow, or joy he heard? Would he find relevance in what was said? Would he relate to what the person was experiencing? The road to Emmaus story shows him doing all those things for his bereaved friends. When you view troubled participants with eyes of compassion, they experience the love of God and its healing power.

How do you help someone who constantly interrupts others?

As a facilitator, try not to label participants, but it is important to note behavior. A season may come when a participant takes over the group by frequently interrupting others with lengthy comments about their own situation. The behavior may be rooted in enthusiasm, poor social skills, a lifelong character quirk, or lack of understanding of the ground rules of group process.

Confer with your partner to assess what is going on. Is the group bothered by the zealous participant, or do they accept one another as they are and make light of disruptive behavior? If the latter is true, the disturbances usually disappear as the person gets comfortable with the group. On the other hand, when interruptions by one participant (let's call him "John") disrupt the flow of sharing, you need to act. If you don't, participants may resent John, and confrontations occur. Sometimes meeker participants stop sharing or quit the group.

Review group etiquette, emphasizing taking turns and respectful listening. If a disruptive incident follows, I might apply the rules by saying, "We appreciate your enthusiasm, John, but now it's Joan's turn to speak." Also be mindful of what triggers John's contributions. Eye contact with the facilitator is enough for some participants to start talking. To test that notion, choose a seat at the next session that keeps John out of your line of vision. It could solve the problem. If not, have a teammate with you if you decide to take John aside to discuss his habit of interrupting others. It's risky, but if it's done with respect and care for him plus openness to God's will, the disruptive behavior generally improves.

Does Seasons of Hope focus on Church issues?

Seasons of Hope faith sharing focuses on Christ and the personal concerns of the bereaved. Scripture isn't dissected there. The Word is proclaimed to open everyone to Christ, not to preach about how anyone should feel or act. If topics such as theology, Church practices, or issues in the headlines arise, speak with your pastoral advisor and arrange a visit to address questions.

Do you follow up with participants between sessions?

Decide with your teammates whether to minister by phone between sessions. Some teams like to call everyone. We contact participants who are having a "bad" week or are absent without notice. Sometimes a call of concern brings a person back the next week.

Are participants encouraged to contact each other between sessions?

Yes, absolutely! We encourage on-site folks to record and use contact information they gather in the Network Directory of the *Journal.* Online participants who tell us to share their email address receive the addresses of other interested participants.

What if participants want to continue after their fourth season?

By the time someone is ready for a new year of seasons, the group will most likely have different members and the person will be at a different point on their grief journey. So the content takes on new meaning and is just as comforting. Healing unfolds more slowly for some people than others. Don't be surprised if some long timers are destined for a spot on your team. If so, it's a blessing.

How can facilitators avoid taking on too much?

Ministering to the bereaved is a very rewarding experience, but it takes physical, emotional, and spiritual energy. The compassion you so freely shower on those who mourn is essential for you as well. Be kind to yourself. Keep your sense of humor, especially when everything doesn't go as planned.

How do you minister without exhausting yourself? Three things are important:

- Set your priorities.
- Know your limits.
- Don't take on problems that don't belong to you.

That means you have to say no on occasion. Your choices will keep you in ministry or drive you from it.

Your calling asks you to do your best for the bereaved and to leave the rest to the Lord. He will heal the brokenhearted when they are ready. Try to keep your eyes on Christ through prayer, reflection, and an occasional spiritual retreat. Trust that he will give you what you need to minister. Besides spiritual stamina, his help often comes through supportive clergy and other parish staff members, teammates, and family who willingly journey with you.

Is there ongoing support for Seasons of Hope facilitators?

Yes! Our Seasons of Hope facilitator-enrichment series of videos and webinars helps sharpen your ministry leadership skills and builds upon the essential spiritual and practical advice of this

Leader's Guide. The series, plus a variety of program resources is available at www.avemariapress.com/products/seasons-of-hope-facilitators-pack.

The Benefit of Fellowship

How does fellowship fit into Seasons of Hope?

A fellowship break encourages the bereaved to socialize with one another and the ministry team when sessions are held on-site at a facility. The break can occur during the sign-in period, before faith sharing, or after the final prayer. Through mingling informally, participants get to know each other as neighbors and members of the community. Setting aside the loneliness that they may be experiencing, participants can relax, enjoy each other, and build the community of faith.

How is fellowship accomplished in online sessions?

We don't include a fellowship break online because informal mingling isn't possible. In the computer screen's gallery view, no conversation is private. But we do find that participants get to know each other as neighbors during the Opening icebreakers and when God-wink moments and favorite items are shared.

What's next?

Now that you have explored the essence of faith sharing, facilitating, and the benefits of fellowship, the next chapter explains how to host weekly sessions.

Four

About Weekly Sessions

When you think of sessions as encounters with the Lord, preparation takes on new meaning. Jesus's friend Martha prepared a gathering in his honor, but she was too busy serving to enjoy his company (Lk 10:38–42). Jesus truly appreciated Martha's hospitality, but he reminded her that her sister Mary's focus on him was the better part. Just as he befriended Martha and Mary, Jesus has befriended you. Because he consoles you in your grief, you can serve others who mourn. Let your preparation honor him.

To help you minister, the first part of this chapter explains how to plan for successful sessions. It has basic information for both on-site and online offerings, noting some variations. The rest of the chapter helps the weekly process come alive and includes an activity checklist that the team can use to organize an on-site session. If an online offering is planned, also read chapter 5, "About Online Sessions," which includes a facilitator/host checklist.

Planning Ahead

(four weeks to one week before a season begins)

Schedule a planning meeting with your teammates to go over the details of the season. Most teams look at a season as a whole and then review the needs of individual sessions.

What's a quick way to see a whole season?

Review the Sessions-at-a-Glance tables in the appendix for the season you are preparing (these tables begin on page 160). It's a must-have for your planning meeting and will be helpful to reference as you read the information that follows. Look across a row for a session's

- title
- theme

- opening time allotment
- scripture citation, reflection activity, and time allotment
- faith-sharing focus and time allotment
- summary and fellowship time allotment

Look down a column to see how the season handles one of these components. The Activity column, for example, lists the scripture passage for each session, optional music, and what participants do to reflect on God.

How are seasons alike?

Every season follows a familiar six-week pattern of sessions with these titles:

Session 1: Point of Departure
Session 2: Path to Understanding
Session 3: Obstacles on the Journey
Session 4: Path to Inner Healing
Session 5: Way of Suffering
Session 6: Final Destination

From season to season, sessions are conducted in the same manner. You always welcome the group, give the session's title and theme, and pray the Seasons of Hope Prayer, available on page 72 of this *Leader's Guide* and the back cover of each *Journal*. You then read scripture and do a simple activity focused on Christ, have a time of faith sharing, summarize the session and point out group accomplishments, then close the session in prayer for the deceased. A time of unstructured fellowship is also part of on-site sessions.

How do seasons differ?

Each season offers fresh themes, scripture, and ways to find Christ. Compare the four Sessions-at-a-Glance tables in the appendix for details.

How do themes fit in?

Drawn from scripture, a theme shows the focus of a session. It may address confusion, memories of loved ones, lost dreams, fear, hope, searching for joy and consolation, or another issue that conveys the universal nature of suffering and God's concern for those who mourn.

What about time allotments?

Since groups differ, the time suggested in the Sessions-at-a-Glance tables is generally the minimum you can expect to spend. Thirty minutes for fellowship, however, is the maximum. This gives some leeway to reach the weekly goal of two hours on-site or an hour and a half online. After the first session's introduction to the program, the Opening is for icebreakers and items participants find helpful. The Activity segment shares a scripture story, offers personal time to reflect on the passage, and paves the way for faith sharing. Use the Footprint to pace each session.

What is a Footprint?

A Footprint is the blueprint for a weekly session, whether it is on-site or online. Not only does it help you plan a nurturing meeting environment, but its script gives the words to conduct the session. The Sessions-at-a-Glance tables in the appendix are outlines of the six Footprints of each season. Part 2 of this *Leader's Guide*, which begins on page 71, contains the twenty-four Footprints. Refer to one of them as you read the rest of this chapter.

Do participants receive a Footprint?

No. Participants receive a *Journal* booklet that has the Seasons of Hope Prayer, a Guidepost page, Marking the Route exercise for each session, and Soul Work to do between sessions (see chapter 6, "About Seasons of Hope *Journals*").

What do you look at first to plan a season?

Focus on the items-needed list in the Footprints, noting those used on-site versus online. Some items create a welcoming atmosphere while others bring Christ into focus. Then consider optional items. The Activity shows how options can be used in the different sessions. Decide with your teammates whether to add them to the basic reflection activities.

Where do you find things from the items-needed list?

Items such as a bell, a crucifix, and rosary are common to our homes. You can borrow other items from a parish ministry. For example, the faith formation ministry for youth probably has colored paper and markers to share. The liturgy committee might have extra Stations of the Cross booklets, incense, a crown of thorns from a youth passion play, or Jesus prayer cards. Bibles may be found in facility classrooms or borrowed from the parish library or faith formation office.

Each season has different needs. Give yourself enough time to gather on-site items, especially if you need to purchase or order something.

What items will you use each week?

Each session the bare essentials you will use are a spiritual focal point display, Bibles, boxes of tissues, a Seasons of Hope *Leader's Guide* for each facilitator, and a *Journal* booklet for each group member, facilitator, and helper. Pre-session music is also recommended, which means you will need a music player of some sort. Do a sound check to be sure whatever device you use has volume capacity suitable for the space. A tablet or cell phone may need an additional speaker, for example.

Why is music played before sessions?

Sacred music creates a mood in which participants can put their worries aside. What better way to open hearts and minds to scripture and God's consolation? A variety of spiritual music is available on CDs or various apps. (See the Suggested Sound Recordings and Sacred Images section in the appendix.) If your team needs a music player, check out what's available in your facility meeting space or borrow from the music or youth ministry.

What focal point display is suggested?

To center participants on Jesus during prayer and reflection, my favorite focal point is a framed image of the Sacred Heart of Jesus beside some votive candles. Choose a sacred image of our Lord that appeals to you. You might also use small sculptures or statues. As themes change, you can add a relevant sacred symbol. Just be certain to keep the image of Christ prominent.

How will Bibles be used?

Everyone at Seasons of Hope reads along when the scripture is proclaimed. A Bible is also used at home to review the scripture passage of the week during Soul Work. It's okay for participants to have different versions of the Bible. Wording may vary, but the message comes through.

You can provide Bibles during on-site sessions, if desired. If you ask participants to bring their own, have a couple on hand for those who forget to bring one.

How is the *Journal* used?

Each participant uses a *Journal* during sessions and at home. Facilitators and helpers should each have one to use during the session, too. The *Journal* gives quick access to the Seasons of Hope Prayer; the Guidepost, which gives the title, theme, and scripture citation for each session; and Marking the Route, which has the reflection activity. You can also use the booklet to point out Soul Work exercises to do at home.

Is the chair arrangement for the on-site session something you should discuss in advance?

Yes. The more decisions your team can make before the first session the better. Here are some options for placing chairs in the room.

1. Everyone sits in a circle for opening remarks, scripture reading, the exercises, and faith sharing. Put the focal point display on a low table in the center of the chairs so that everyone can see it. The facilitator sits with the group but can stand at a lectern to share opening statements and instructions from the Footprint in this *Leader's Guide*.
2. The group sits at a table, preferably so that everyone is in view and earshot and can see the focal point display. This works for a group of eight or fewer, including the team. If a large conference table must be used, space the chairs evenly so that no one is isolated.

A table makes handling booklets and drinks convenient, but it has a downside. Participants who get emotional or need to leave the group for a few moments often won't budge because backing away from the table calls attention to them.

3. The group moves as different phases of the session occur. As participants gather, chairs are in rows (parted at the middle, if desired) facing the focal point display and the facilitator. After opening remarks, the scripture reading, and the meditation/written activity, the group forms a circle for faith sharing that begins and ends at the focal point display. Subgroups also gather around a display.

Each approach works. I particularly like the third option because participants quietly focus on the Lord before literally facing the group for faith sharing. They have to work together to make a circle, and in the process they stretch, chat, and gain a new perspective on the gathering. Regrouping stirs up energy—a good place for faith sharing to begin.

For on-site programs in a parish facility, is it advisable to make an inspection visit first?

Yes. The best way to plot out the room for greeting, session activities, and fellowship is to make a team visit well before sessions begin. A diagram (floor plan) of the room may be available from the building manager, or you can draw one. Use it to sketch where you want a lectern, chairs, and tables for welcoming participants, the focal point display, music equipment, and refreshments. The appearance of the room will send a message; let it be one of hospitality.

If a custodian will prepare the room for sessions, go over the diagram with them during the planning stage. While there, check out the room. Is there enough furniture for the group? What about a stand (lectern)? Are extension cords needed for electrical outlets? Does the kitchen have appliances to heat water and brew coffee? Check the supply of coffee (perhaps decaf, depending on time of day), tea bags, cream, sugar, and honey. Is ice available? What about water pitchers, paper goods, utensils, linens, and other hospitality items?

Should the team discuss hospitality plans for sessions?

It's wise to include hospitality on the agenda of your planning meeting. Start with materials for the welcome process. Then focus on how the team will greet participants. Once the details are decided, divide the tasks with your teammates on the Team Activity Checklist (page 53) and keep the plan handy for the first session.

What materials do you need to welcome participants to sessions?

Basic items include "Welcome to Seasons of Hope" signs, a roster with names of participants and columns to check each week during sign-in, pencils, name tags, markers, and *Journals*. Be sure to have extra enrollment forms for drop-ins the first and second weeks or to use if advance enrollment did not occur.

If a welcome table will be used, discuss whether to add a tablecloth, welcome sign, and decorations of the season. Since participants like to know who is in charge, consider unique name tags for the ministry team.

For sessions at a home, what should be considered?

Decide how to greet participants. Will you post a "Welcome to Seasons of Hope" sign outside so participants know it's the place? Who will be at the front door? Will any group members need assistance getting from car to meeting room?

For sessions at a parish facility, what should be considered?

Creating a welcoming atmosphere is equally important in the parish setting. Each week we put a "Welcome to Seasons of Hope" sign at the entrance. When long, winding corridors lead to the room, we mark the way for the first couple of weeks. Simple 8.5" × 11" sheets, handwritten or computer generated, serve the purpose. Just remember tacks or tape for posting.

A personal welcome at the entrance is ideal. If possible, station someone at the door thirty minutes before the session begins. Pick the most outgoing teammate with a ready smile and a knack for putting people at ease. If a team member isn't available, ask a friend to lend a hand.

Is a welcome table necessary at a parish facility?

A welcome table is useful for the first week or two to greet and register participants, distribute *Journals*, and assist latecomers. Thereafter, a greeter can handle the sign-in sheets for attendance and refreshments, offer name tags, and receive any donated refreshments for the session.

What about refreshments?

The team should discuss whether to donate snacks or purchase them through the parish. Will participants contribute? If so, will a sign-up sheet be used? How will contributions be acknowledged? Also discuss the refreshment table. Where will it be? Will one teammate receive and prepare items, or will it be a team effort?

An on-site group that meets after daily Mass or at dinnertime might schedule the fellowship break before the program begins. Mid-morning and afternoon groups often break before faith sharing. And programs that conclude at noon often offer refreshments and fellowship last.

Teamwork for the Weekly Sessions

Once the program is planned, what's next?

The success of each session begins well before participants arrive. Discuss what each teammate will do on the days of sessions. The following questions define roles.

What will the facilitator do on the day of the session?

The facilitator sets up and cleans the room with other members of the team. But don't get caught up in the work like Jesus's friend Martha. As participants arrive, help them feel welcome. Then use the Footprint as a guide to move the session along at a reasonable pace.

What if a pastor or another parish staff member attends?

If your pastor or other pastoral staff member can get involved, they might want to help welcome everyone, introduce the team, lead prayer, and share in facilitating the group. Whatever this person contributes will enhance the group's journey together.

What will teammates do?

The team works together to set up and clean up, distribute Bibles, proclaim the Word, help with activities, facilitate or assist during faith sharing, take charge of refreshments, and mingle with participants during the fellowship break. In other words, teamwork is why Seasons of Hope succeeds.

What happens just before each session?

When you and your teammates prepare the meeting place, also prepare yourselves. Pray together in Jesus's name and ask God to inspire you and those who come. The session Footprint lets you facilitate with confidence. Here are additional tips on the process.

Using the Footprints

1. Opening

Who gets the session going?

The responsibility to begin the session lies with the facilitator even when the pastor or another pastoral staff member is present.

How does the Footprint indicate what is to be said or presented during the session?

The Opening and Summary segments use bullets to prompt you to share specific information with the group. Some Footprint instructions are geared to the site of the group and are shown in bold and parentheses—**(On-site)** or **(Online)**. Throughout the Footprint a bold heading—**Script**—indicates when to present the text that follows.

What does the initial welcome involve?

The welcome reflects a spirit of hospitality and love for our brothers and sisters in Christ, many of whom are strangers to us. It takes courage for each person to come to the first session of the program, so acknowledge that bravery and let the participants know that the team is glad they came!

How formal should team introductions be?

Each ministry team's personality comes out in the introductions. Decide together how to handle the introductions. Will the team be together at the lectern or sitting with the group? Will they share anything besides their names with participants? Even though some getting acquainted happens beforehand, be certain to formally introduce all team members.

Is there a specific prayer for Seasons of Hope?

Yes. For ease of use, the Seasons of Hope Prayer is printed on the back cover of each *Journal*. On-site groups pray it out loud together each week. For online groups, a teammate usually offers the prayer aloud while others pray along silently. That avoids transmission issues.

How are participant introductions handled?

The Footprint offers guidance. Some people choke up in a new group, and others feel compelled to talk at length. Neither way gets the first session off on the right foot. So ease into introductions during the first session by keeping it simple: their name and their relation to the deceased. Assure participants that naming their departed loved one and more details will be shared in a few minutes.

How do you present the details of Seasons of Hope to the group?

The Footprint makes it easy. The simple way is to use the Script from the first session's Opening. To build confidence in presenting, practice reading the text aloud beforehand. If you'd rather improvise, use the *Journal* to go over the program's Christ-centered themes and the exercises and Soul Work done at home. Be sure to include the concept of peer ministry and any housekeeping concerns.

What does housekeeping involve?

"Housekeeping" refers to miscellaneous announcements that range from location of the restrooms to schedule changes to need for transportation by one of the participants.

What helps participants get comfortable with sharing?

During the Opening, we invite everyone, including the team, to give us a peek into their life since the last session. We ask for a God wink (a surprising personal experience gratefully received as a divine gift), an insight from the *Journal* Soul Work done at home, or a favorite faith- or grief-related item. Participants discover they are among like-minded friends, and that makes the faith sharing that follows extra special.

2. Activity

What happens during the Activity?

The weekly theme comes alive as you share words of introduction and a teammate reads the scripture story. Then have participants turn to Marking the Route in the *Journal* and review the directions for the reflection exercise. Sometimes sacred music is played softly during this time. Pausing to privately reflect on the scripture opens participants to Jesus's message for them and can inspire the faith sharing that follows.

Why do teammates proclaim the Word?

Although participants are certainly capable, the team is ideal for proclaiming the scripture passages. It provides an opportunity to involve a teammate in a very specific way and helps ensure that the reading is well prepared and proclaimed. Additionally, participants don't have to worry about being called upon at random to read aloud for the whole group.

What if participants have never used a Bible?

Thanks to Vatican II, many Catholics are now avid Bible readers, but not everyone is. If someone needs help finding the passage, give them a hand. Be sure everyone has ample time to locate the page before proceeding.

Are theories of grief and grieving formally presented?

No. Seasons of Hope emphasizes the spiritual side of mourning and finding consolation in Jesus Christ. Yet the spectrum of grief reactions isn't ignored. In telling their stories, participants reveal a range of grief-related emotions and reactions. The *Journal* appendix offers a Helpful Resources section for participants interested in exploring grief theory and the psychology of loss.

3. Faith Sharing

Chapter 3 gives a lengthy discussion on the fine art of facilitating a faith-sharing group. Here are some additional practical concerns.

What about group etiquette?

Without ground rules, the faith-sharing time becomes a free-for-all. Participants need to know what a facilitator does and what is expected of them. Have participants turn to the Guide to Group Etiquette in the appendix of the *Journal* when you explain the rules. Return to that page each week if needed.

PART 1

What do you do if a cofacilitator is unavailable?

You can facilitate a group solo if you have to, but ask a dependable participant to signal when it's ten minutes before the end of the session. This will help you finish on time.

4. Summary

Although this phase has the least amount of time allotted for it, it is important.

How do you wrap up the session?

You might share an insight you gained from the session or challenge everyone to think of a discovery they made. Another approach is to give your impression of the group's journey together. If faith-sharing subgroups were formed, you can invite a volunteer from each one to offer a brief summary of where their group went with their faith sharing. Then add your insights on the overall accomplishments of the session.

Are there Summary announcements?

Yes. Encourage participants to look forward to the next session by giving its theme and mentioning any special item they need to bring. Plus, remind everyone to complete the weekly session by doing the Soul Work in the *Journal*.

Do participants have the prayer used in the Summary?

No. The facilitator, the pastor, or a pastoral staff member prays the Prayer to the Giver of Hope aloud and asks participants to pray silently for the souls of their deceased loved ones.

How do you get formal feedback on a season?

Have participants complete the Season Survey at the last session of each season. It is in each Seasons of Hope *Journal* (see the appendix) and is also available in a printable form at www.avemariapress.com/products/seasons-of-hope-facilitators-pack. The survey can give tangible proof of how God blesses your efforts.

5. Fellowship Break

How much time is allotted for the fellowship break?

A two-hour on-site session could have up to thirty minutes for the fellowship break. Sometimes participants take a while to get comfortable with each other, but when they do, a sense of camaraderie and parish community evolves. We find such bonding is also possible for online groups that don't have a planned break. The Opening icebreakers—God winks, Soul Work insights, and favorite items segments—add the humor, history, and kindred spirit that's so essential to community building.

Is there an easy way to remember all the details?

The following checklist comes in handy. It sums up the weekly process described in this chapter.

Team Activity Checklist

Before the Session

____ Read the Footprint and scripture passage for the week.
____ Gather items needed (listed in the Footprint).

Day of Session

1 hour before Opening:

____ Meet at the location and pray together.
____ Set up chairs, tissue boxes, lectern (optional), welcome table, focal point display, music equipment, refreshments, and signs.

30 minutes before Opening:

____ Greet participants.
____ Help with sign-in and name tags (weekly).
____ Distribute *Journals* (session 1).

5 minutes before Opening:

____ Join participants (a teammate stays at welcome table to greet late arrivals).

Opening: 5–20 minutes (changes weekly)

Facilitator

____ Use a Footprint to lead the session.
____ Welcome everyone and state the session's title and theme.
____ Introduce the team.
____ Lead the Seasons of Hope Prayer using the *Journal.*
____ Seek information on participants noted on the Footprint.
____ Give program details (session 1).
____ Invite participants to share God winks, Soul Work insights, or helpful items, books, or community resources (sessions 2–6).
____ Share housekeeping details.

Activity: 15–35 minutes (changes weekly)

Facilitator

_____ Present the script about the scripture passage.
_____ Invite a teammate to read the scripture passage.
_____ Complete the script that follows the reading.
_____ Give Activity instructions (participants refer to Marking the Route in the *Journal*).

Teammate

_____ Read scripture.
_____ Assist with materials for activities.

Faith Sharing: 25–50 minutes (changes weekly)

Facilitator

_____ Explain ground rules and go over group etiquette guidelines in the *Journal* (session 1).
_____ Pose Footprint questions to the group and encourage faith sharing.

Teammate

_____ Act as quiet partner.
_____ Share in group discussion.

Summary: 5 minutes

Facilitator

_____ Have subgroups, if any, report highlights of faith sharing.
_____ Summarize accomplishments of the day.
_____ Remind participants to complete *Journal* Soul Work at home.
_____ Announce the theme of the next session.
_____ Offer the Prayer to the Giver of Hope.

Fellowship Break: up to 30 minutes (at scheduled time)

Team

_____ Socialize with participants.
_____ Circulate refreshment sign-up sheet, if desired.

After the Session

Team

_____ Put the space back in order.

____ Discuss group dynamics.
____ Look forward to the next session.

At this point, you have the general knowledge you need to conduct an on-site Seasons of Hope session with a Footprint from part 2 of the *Leader's Guide*. The next chapter focuses on how to conduct successful online sessions.

Five

About Online Sessions

Years ago, when Seasons of Hope was in its infancy, the idea of an online faith-sharing group for bereaved Catholics was beyond imagining. Now the unimaginable is possible. But it took the worldwide pandemic that brought parish life to a halt and skyrocketed the number of bereft parishioners to get us facilitators to even consider going online with the groups.

Admittedly, I was among the early footdraggers. Questions flooded in. Would anyone sign up? How difficult is hosting online? Would the program work as well? My teammates had the same concerns. Fear of the unknown enters into any decision in ministry, doesn't it? Yet Jesus encourages us to prayerfully ask for what we need (Mt 7:7–8). He assures us that when we knock seeking his guidance, the door will be opened. We took his teaching to heart. In the process of going beyond our comfort zone, we discovered the online option is well worth considering.

The first part of this chapter can help you and your team discern whether a Seasons of Hope online group would be a good addition to what you offer on-site for your parish. Based on our positive experience with Zoom (a videoconferencing software), this chapter explains what you need for online sessions, the benefits and drawbacks, and how to plan for success. The second part of the chapter gives helpful tips that keep sessions flowing smoothly and provides an activity checklist that can be used to fine-tune a session to the online setting.

Where to Start

What are the initial steps to set up the online program?

Confirm whether everyone on the team has access to the internet and a device that supports video communication. Then talk with your pastoral advisor to see if the parish is already a licensed user of videoconferencing software. If so, investigate whether the Seasons of Hope team can be added to the parish's account as "users" for the purpose of conducting online sessions.

If the parish has not yet invested in such software, you will need to research the various videoconferencing platforms yourself. Check out Zoom and its many competitors to find the platform that best meets your needs. Be sure your choice is user friendly and secure; has advance scheduling, waiting rooms, breakout rooms, and screen sharing; and fits the length of your sessions. Get pastoral approval for the cost of the new software. Decide whether you or a team helper will be the online host. Review and edit the account settings to meet the needs of your sessions.

What preparation does an online host need?

Check out the website of the communication platform you will be using. It should give you access to expert-led tutorials, training classes, and short video demonstrations on the uses of the platform. Other video tutorials on the internet can help, too. Once you have the basics down, schedule some practice meetings online with family, friends, or teammates to build your confidence.

What are the benefits of online groups?

There are numerous benefits to having sessions online. You won't have to book a parish or diocesan hall, set up or clean up a meeting room, or tend to refreshments. You won't have to gather name tags, markers, pencils, sign-in sheets, welcome signs, table covers, and tissues. When inclement weather creates unsafe travel conditions, participants are safe at home. Any concerns about driving to or from sessions after dark are eliminated. If public health issues require masks and social distancing indoors, online programs are not affected. And the team and participants can access sessions even when they live or travel outside the area.

What are the drawbacks?

Online sessions cost more. If the parish does not have a video communication license in place, you will need to purchase one that fits the length of the sessions. Mailing *Journals* also adds expense. Your groups will be limited to individuals who have internet access, a device that supports video communication, and confidence in their ability to access an online session. At least one team member must be trained to navigate the controls to host sessions and be able to troubleshoot when others need assistance. The usual roles of other team members have to be adjusted to the new setting. And online sessions lack opportunities for private conversations, which affects team communication and socializing among the group members.

Can you combine on-site and online sessions?

It can be done when a parish facility has the means to project the images and voices of participants whether they are present in the meeting room or appear on the video screen. If the acoustics in the room make hearing difficult for those who are listening online, have a handheld microphone available for the on-site participants.

Planning for Success

Once your parish commits to the online approach, here are some things to discuss with your team.

How much time does an online session take?

Plan on an hour and a half to comfortably complete a session online.

How is promotion of Seasons of Hope affected?

Be sure that promotional materials, recruitment announcements, and sign-up forms reflect the online option and its shortened session length. Before enrollment begins, decide whether *Journals* will be mailed to online participants or available for pickup. Place your booklet order with that schedule in mind.

Is the enrollment process different for online sessions?

Although the enrollment process remains the same, you will want to ask potential participants some extra questions. Do they have internet access? A computer, tablet, or phone that supports video communication? Experience with online meetings? Many people are familiar with videoconferencing, but you may need to recommend a tutorial video that shows how to join a meeting. You can also invite the person to join you or the host for some practice with the online system before Seasons of Hope begins. And be sure to tell participants whether their *Journal* will be mailed or available for pickup.

What if a potential participant does not have the technology or ability to use the necessary devices?

Offer the person the option to complete the booklet exercises independently and have a weekly phone call from a team member. This tends to the person's spiritual side of grieving and conveys the message that their faith community cares.

What about providing access to the Bible?

For participants who don't own a Bible, you can refer them to the US Conference of Catholic Bishops website (https://Bible.usccb.org/Bible) for free access to an online Catholic Bible. To make things even easier for them, you can look up each session's scripture passage and copy its web address into an email message to send to participants. The participants can then click on the links you have provided in the email to access the scripture readings.

Does going online change the role of the facilitator?

It does. When you are both the facilitator and online host, besides keeping the session flowing, you issue email invitations, and use the controls to admit people to sessions, create breakout rooms, share music or visuals, and troubleshoot glitches. When someone else on the team is the online host, you facilitate the group process and let your teammate know when to navigate the controls.

What is the role of a team helper for online sessions?

With the online approach, a team helper will join in welcoming participants and may offer the Seasons of Hope Prayer for the group, proclaim the scripture passage, share helpful grief and faith items, assist the facilitator during faith sharing, and help the online host with troubleshooting as needed.

What is the welcoming process online?

To ensure that each participant receives a warm welcome, enable the waiting room option for your sessions. With it, no one pops into the session unannounced; instead, each person is admitted by the host and cordially greeted by all the team and participants present.

What about using music online?

The selected sacred music is an important part of many sessions. It's best to use your computer's music app and the videoconferencing software's advanced Share Screen feature for music. That way you have full use of your microphone and camera as the music streams.

What about displaying an image of Jesus as a focal point?

The display is a powerful reminder that we gather to focus on our relationship with the Lord during grieving. A simple way to encourage that mindset online is to ask participants to have their favorite sacred artwork of the Lord or a Jesus prayer card on hand during each session. We send a Jesus prayer card with each booklet.

Are Footprint exercises different online?

Only one session out of twenty-four has a different Marking the Route exercise to use online. All Footprints in part 2 have both on-site and online exercises.

Why is the fellowship break optional online?

Fellowship breaks aim to encourage one-on-one conversations, but we found that multiple simultaneous conversations transmitted online become inaudible babble. Nevertheless, you might want to schedule a brief break for participants to pause from interacting with the group. It's an option that would not foster fellowship but may meet the personal needs of your group.

Once the new season is planned for online gathering, what's next?

Session Invitations

How do you invite participants and team members to sessions?

Use your communication platform's account portal to schedule a session and enter its details. The site creates a meeting invitation which you copy and email to group members. On the day of the session, they click on the "join" link in the email invitation. Depending on your account settings, they may also need to enter a meeting ID and passcode when prompted. For each session, you create and send a new email invitation.

Helpful Tips to Keep Online Sessions Flowing Smoothly

What do you do as the facilitator and host to start a session?

About thirty minutes before a session, open the videoconferencing app and go to the portal where you scheduled the meeting. Locate the session and click on the start button. This will begin the video feed. Be sure that audio is also enabled. Enlarge the meeting video on your screen and make sure your image is visible to participants. Test the microphone. Is the waiting room feature enabled? If so, click on the Participants icon. It will show you a blank column that will eventually list the names of those waiting to be admitted. Want to use the Share Screen feature? Then have the desired files already open on your desktop. And be sure to have your session materials within reach.

When does the rest of the team arrive?

Most teams plan to meet before participants arrive. It's a chance to pray together, go over assignments, test the sound level of session music, and cover any last-minute details. When it's time to admit group members, the whole team is present and ready to welcome them.

What happens while participants gather for the session?

As the team members greet new arrivals, they also encourage and join in informal group chatter. Less talkative groups appreciate listening to soft sacred music as they wait for the session to begin.

Are technology issues common among inexperienced participants?

Sure. Expect a phone call, email, or text message when access issues occur. You can send another meeting invitation to those who cannot find theirs. You can offer suggestions on the proper steps to get into the session. And you might have to do some friendly coaching during the program when someone unwittingly disables their audio or video feed. Glitches like these may delay the program, but they often create a sense of camaraderie that bonds the group.

Session Footprints

Do Footprints contain special directions for hosting online groups?

Yes. Woven into the usual session scripts, each Footprint includes prompts shown as **(Online)** that are followed by specific information or technical directions for the online host.

What about Opening comments online?

You still set the tone of each session by sharing the title and theme noted in the Footprint. That way the scripture focus of the week is emphasized.

What about the Seasons of Hope Prayer?

Praying out loud together as a group is wonderful on-site, but multiple electronic devices do not always transmit voices in perfect synchrony. It helps to test the sound in advance with teammates. If there's a problem, have one team member read the prayer aloud while everyone else silently follows along with the booklet.

Is anything different with introductions?

With on-site groups, introductions usually proceed in an orderly fashion up and down rows or around a circle of chairs. With an online gallery view, however, different devices may put participant images in different patterns. One way to avoid confusion of who goes next is to suggest that participants raise their hand or click on the "raised hand" emoji (picture symbol) on the screen to signal that they are ready to speak. Make sure no one is left out before you proceed with the rest of the Opening.

Are there any different housekeeping suggestions for the online group?

Since Seasons of Hope is an interactive process, encourage participants to keep their video feed on throughout the session. That way no one loses an opportunity to engage with the group. They should, however, feel free to temporarily mute their microphone on the meeting controls if it gets noisy where they are. If the online sessions will include a fellowship break, inform the group during week one. To encourage networking, offer to create and distribute a list of names and email addresses of those in the group who want to share contact information.

What about sharing helpful resources?

Encourage participants and the team to share items that lift the spirit and help them better understand their grief. Items can be read aloud or shown for everyone to see on the video feed.

Is there any change to the Activity segment?

The Footprint script is used in the usual manner, and a team member still proclaims the scripture passage. Any online-specific exercise is included in its Footprint and corresponding *Journal*.

How is faith sharing impacted in an online session?

Online you get to clearly see someone's face and the movement of their lips. That, plus volume control, helps everyone hear what is said, which often isn't the case in a classroom. Some may signal with a "raised hand" emoji when they want to speak, but most participants simply speak up or nod.

Does faith sharing benefit from breakout rooms?

Breakout rooms are recommended if you have more than one facilitator and a group of ten or more. The breakout room feature gives everyone more time to share their faith stories. Plus, it lets you group participants by type of loss, if desired. Be sure to indicate in the breakout room settings the amount of time allotted for faith sharing. That way the groups are automatically returned to the main meeting room for the Summary.

If a problem arises, a facilitator or participant can contact you by the chat feature, which sends you a typed message. To address the problem, you can respond via chat or join that breakout room.

Are there any changes in the Summary?

If breakout rooms are used, it is good to have a teammate or participant from each room share highlights from their group's faith sharing. Otherwise, the session conclusion remains the same.

What about the closing prayer?

Read the Prayer to the Giver of Hope while the group listens and prays silently. Conclude the session with the Sign of the Cross.

What happens with the Season Survey?

You can email the Word document version of the Season Survey with the last session's meeting invitation. Ask participants to type their responses on it and email it back before the session. Or allot time during the session to complete the survey and return it by email. The Season Survey is available at https://www.avemariapress.com/products/seasons-of-hope-facilitators-pack.

Is there an easy way to remember all the details?

Yes. The following checklist builds upon the weekly process of Seasons of Hope groups described in chapter 4. It focuses on successfully using technology to keep your online sessions flowing smoothly. A printable checklist is also available at the Seasons of Hope page at avemariapress.com.

Facilitator and Host Activity Checklist

Day before the Session

____ Copy session invitation from Zoom meeting page and email to group.

Day of Session

30 minutes before Opening:

____ Open the video feed.
____ Admit and welcome teammates to the pre-session meeting.
____ Pray together, seeking God's guidance for the session.
____ Review sound and clarity of optional music with the team.
____ Review team assignments.
____ Share any participant updates.

10 minutes before Opening:

____ Start background music with Share Screen, if desired.
____ Admit people in the waiting room to the meeting room and greet them as they enter.
____ Correct names on the screen via the Participants column.
____ Tend to any participant access issues.

Opening

____ Turn off the background music and Share Screen.
____ Welcome everyone and state the session's title and theme.
____ Invite a teammate to read the Seasons of Hope Prayer.
____ Talk about the microphone and video controls (session 1).
____ Explain how to signal the intent to speak during introductions (session 1).
____ Use Share Screen if needed during exchange of helpful items.
____ Review program and housekeeping items (session 1).

Activity

____ Post the session's scripture passage on Share Screen, if desired.
____ Invite a teammate to read the scripture passage.
____ Use the Share Screen advanced feature to play music.
____ Assign breakout rooms for the Exercise (session 1).
____ Receive participants returning from breakout rooms (session 1).

Faith Sharing

_____ Create breakout rooms when appropriate.
_____ Respond to messages from breakout rooms via chat or a visit.

Summary

_____ Read the Prayer to the Giver of Hope for the group.
_____ Allot time to complete Season Survey and email to you (session 6).

After the Session

_____ Meet with teammates to acknowledge their contributions and review group dynamics.
_____ Plan team assignments for the next session.

A chapter and a checklist. That's a lot of information that will become second nature once you host your first online session. I was surprised to find that it was much easier than I expected. If I can do it, so can you! Just ask the Lord to bless your Seasons of Hope groups wherever they gather. Trust in him. And faithfully use the Footprints from part 2 of this *Leader's Guide*.

The next chapter completes part 1 of the *Leader's Guide* by exploring the use of the Seasons of Hope *Journals*.

Six

About Seasons of Hope *Journals*

The *Journal* booklets are an integral part of Seasons of Hope. Each of the four seasons has its own booklet for the team and participants to use during on-site and online sessions. And with the *Journal's* home exercises, participants can independently keep their focus on the spiritual side of mourning between sessions. To help you explain the *Journal* to the group and fully utilize it yourself, this chapter presents an overview and the specific components that compose all four booklets.

Why are the *Journals* important?

- The *Journals* save you time by combining session activities into convenient booklets so that you don't have to create or copy handouts.
- *Journals* empower participants. With a new booklet each season, they have details on weekly sessions at their fingertips plus resources on bereavement and the group process.
- *Journals* help participants view their grief through the lens of faith and prepare them for heartfelt faith sharing in the group.
- The *Journal* Soul Work, which is completed at home, continues what a session begins. Its retreat-like approach offers a fresh way to reflect on the scripture story of the week.
- The *Journals* help mourning become a sacred journey in which the bereaved sense God's compassion, mercy, and love in their struggles.

What does each *Journal* contain?

- The Seasons of Hope Prayer
- A welcome page
- Guidepost pages
- Marking the Route exercises
- Soul Work segments for home use

PART 1

- An appendix containing Helpful Resources, a Network Directory, the Guide to Group Etiquette, and a Season Survey
- Acknowledgments

Where is Seasons of Hope explained in the booklet?

The section called Welcome to Seasons of Hope *Journal One* (or other season number) contains an introduction to the program and instructions on how to use the booklet.

What part of the Journal is used every session?

The Seasons of Hope Prayer, the Guidepost page, and Marking the Route exercise are used at each session.

What does the Guidepost provide?

The Guidepost announces each session's title, theme, and scripture reading. Since participants read along in their Bibles at the session, many use the citation given in the Guidepost to locate the scripture passage before the session begins. The Guidepost is used again for Soul Work at home, which calls for another reading of the Word to begin the exercises.

What's in the Marking the Route segment?

Marking the Route describes the activity for the session. You may want participants to read along in the *Journal* as you give instructions. Also point out where to do a writing exercise or take notes. Encourage participants to note whether Marking the Route mentions a special item to bring to the next session—for example, their rosary.

Are questions for faith sharing in the booklets?

No. Faith-sharing questions are listed in the facilitator's Footprint. Participants are encouraged to listen carefully to the questions posed, a practice that fine-tunes their ability to listen to whispers of the soul.

What is the purpose of the Soul Work segment?

Simply put, the *Journal* Soul Work is food for the soul. Participants from the first parish groups, before booklets were a part of the program, asked for something to lift them up between sessions. Soul Work only takes a few minutes each week, but it provides more quality time with the Lord that can bring hope, healing, and consolation.

What are the components of the Soul Work?

- **Looking Back** takes a closer look at the scripture passage presented in the group session and offers another point of view for the participant to contemplate.
- **A Prayer to Find the Way** seeks God's assistance with the grief process.

- **Steps along the Path** uses narrative and exercises to tie the scripture passage into the participant's experience of loss.
- The **Reflection** segment focuses on feelings surrounding loss.
- The **Journal Entry** encourages participants to write their own story. By putting on paper what may go unspoken, we release emotional energy, opening us to God's grace.
- **Moving Forward** recommends a Church ritual (familiar forms of prayer or contemplation) that will aid in the letting go process or asks for a particular act of compassion.
- The **Closing Prayer** offers words of gratitude to God.

Are participants expected to talk about Soul Work at the next session?

No one is required to do so, but during the Opening of each session we ask if anyone would like to share an insight they gained from the previous week's Soul Work. Some may want to talk about one of its prayers that touched their heart or the Moving Forward ritual that brought them comfort.

What is in Helpful Resources?

Helpful Resources offers a list of bereavement books that bring spiritual nourishment through comforting prayer, meditations, and guides to find the way after losing someone special. This section also includes a list of helpful websites to consult for bereavement information, organizations, and publications.

When is the Network Directory introduced and used?

By the third session of the season, participants have grown comfortable with each other, so it's a fitting time to talk about the Network Directory. These pages have space to record names, phone numbers, and email addresses, making it easy for participants to interact outside of sessions. Most participants use the fellowship break or time before a session to gather information. Reaching out to others for support is an important step on the journey of those who are grieving. Online participants can use the booklet to collect contact information shared by email.

What about the Guide to Group Etiquette?

The guide explains the duties of a facilitator and what is expected from group members. The behavior outlined is simply the Golden Rule with examples of basic courtesy. To begin faith sharing at the first session, ask participants to open to the Guide to Group Etiquette in the appendix and review the information. If your group has difficulty with courtesy, return to the guidelines each week and emphasize areas that could improve.

How is the Season Survey used?

This tool helps participants think about their personal experience with Seasons of Hope and offers the team valuable feedback. The open-ended statements give plenty of room for expression. No one is asked to rate the program or the facilitators, but such comments appear occasionally under the "I'd also like to say . . ." statement.

This survey can be completed at home or during the last on-site session. Participants can cut the survey page from the booklet, or you can provide a printable version from www.avemariapress.com. Online participants complete and return the survey that you email to them.

How do participants respond to the Journals?

Our surveys show that participants like the *Journals*. Some are so enthused that they send *Journals* to grief-stricken loved ones and friends who don't have the benefit of our group. I'm always touched by both their compassion and their faith in the *Journal*.

When a former participant wrote to me about the *Journals*, I realized their healing power. She wrote, "My niece died recently, and I want to thank you for the Seasons of Hope *Journals*. They are a blessing. I've been going through them again and have received much comfort."

Do new Journals need to be ordered each season?

Yes. The *Journals* accompany a particular season, so order accordingly. The four *Journals*-at-a-Glance tables in the appendix of this *Leader's Guide* outline what to expect each season.

How else might Seasons of Hope *Journals* be used in consolation ministry?

When a new season is being offered, we provide *Journals* to bereaved homebound parishioners who inquire about the program as well as those whose work schedules interfere with attending on-site or online sessions. Many appreciate a weekly call from us to hear about their insights and grief journey. Some opt to use them independently, and the notes of gratitude that often follow testify to their helpfulness.

You are now ready to embark on the Seasons of Hope ministry. Part 2 follows with its four seasons of Footprints. May your journey with the bereaved bring you ever closer to the Lord!

Part II

Session Footprints

Preamble

Seasons of Hope Prayer

Written from the grieving heart of M. Donna MacLeod, this prayer captures the soul of Seasons of Hope and leads those who mourn to God's tender mercy, love, and consolation.

Our Father,
in this season of sorrow,
we turn to you.
Weakened with sadness,
we shed tears beyond number.
May those you send to help us
bring your love and consolation.

In this season of sorrow,
we lift up our broken hearts to you.
Heal us with your tender mercy
and make this a season of hope.
Trusting in your infinite kindness,
we ask this of you
with the Son and the Holy Spirit.
Amen.

Season One

Session 1

Point of Departure

Theme: For Whom Are You Looking?

On-site items needed:

» sign-in materials (name tags, markers, attendance sheet, and signs)
» Season One *Journals* for group
» pre-session music/player
» focal point (image of Jesus)
» Bibles
» tissue boxes
» timer or watch
» bell (optional)
» refreshment sign-up sheet (optional)

1. Opening (20 minutes)

- On behalf of the team, welcome the group to Session 1: Point of Departure: *For Whom Are You Looking?*
- Begin the session with the Sign of the Cross.
    - **(On-site)** Pray together the Seasons of Hope Prayer on the back cover of the *Journal.*
    - **(Online)** Have a team member offer the Seasons of Hope Prayer aloud while the group joins in silently.

- Keep introductions brief. Invite participants to state their name and relation to their deceased loved one. Give an example: "My name is (Donna), and I lost my (daughter)." Assure them that they will share more during the session.
- Use the script below to explain the Seasons of Hope program, *Journals*, and any housekeeping details.

SEASON One

Script

"Blessed are those who mourn," our Lord assured us, "for they will be comforted" (Mt 5:4). Seasons of Hope brings us together to share in God's love. The support of this community will enable you to give voice to your unique journey and take a step toward healing and spiritual growth.

You are an expert on your grief. We aren't here to teach you about its stages. You meet them on your journey. Instead, we will explore mourning through scripture, prayer, reflection, and faith sharing. We will help you focus on your relationship with the Lord and the many ways his Church offers consolation. Along the way, you will find Jesus in others who mourn and within your own heart.

We use the Bible each week. The *Journal*'s Guidepost page has the Bible citation of the passage you read here and again at home. **(On-site)** Does anyone need to borrow a Bible? *(Have team provide them.)*

Please have your *Journal* handy too. We use it for our opening exercise in group and for Soul Work at home after each session. The Soul Work gives a fresh perspective on the scripture reading. Plus, it allows you to reflect on your relationship with the Lord, write about your loss, and share in a consoling tradition of the Church.

The group session officially concludes with the Summary, which sends you forth with the Prayer to the Giver of Hope.

Now for some housekeeping details:

- We start promptly each week, so please arrive a few minutes early.
- If you can't make a session, please tell us.
- Please silence your cell phone.
- **(Online)** Please mute your speaker if your room gets noisy.
- **(On-site)** Restrooms are located in the . . .
- Each session, you are invited to show one of your favorite faith- or grief-related items. It could be a book, poem, prayer, song, website, devotional item, etc.
- **(On-site)** Fellowship Break is at *(indicate time)*. It's our informal time to share refreshments and get to know each other as neighbors and community members.
- (**On-site** optional) We need help with refreshments. Please sign up to bring one plate of snacks sometime this season. Thank you. This week *(give names)* brought snacks. Let's offer our thanks with a round of applause.

Does anyone have questions?

2. Activity (20 minutes)

Script

Many of us become distraught when someone we love leaves this life. We're in good company. Even the Lord's close friends had difficulty dealing with his death! Let's turn to **John 20:11–18** for an account of Mary Magdalene at the tomb. It gives a compelling view into grief and the confounding path it puts before us. *(Have a teammate read the passage aloud while participants read along in their Bibles.)*

If Mary Magdalene, a faithful disciple who stood at the foot of the Cross on Calvary, let grief blind her to the presence of the risen Jesus, perhaps our preoccupation with our deceased loved ones simply mimics her saintly approach to loss. The first step in her healing was to embrace Jesus and then to share that fateful encounter with others.

Your presence here shows that you seek the Lord, too. The exercise we are about to do is one way to share your faith story. Let's open the *Journal* to Marking the Route for session 1.

Exercise

Script

With a partner, you will complete these statements in your own words:

- My name is ____________________.
- My departed loved one's name is ____________________ .
- His/her death happened ____ weeks/months/years ago.
- The cause of death was . . .
- When he/she died, I was at . . .
- My fondest memory of ______________ is . . .

(On-site) Here's how sharing works:

1. Find a partner—preferably someone you don't know well. *(Continue when pairs are formed.)*
2. Decide who speaks first.
3. You each have about four minutes to tell your story with the statement stems.
4. Listening is an important part of being a participant, so please don't interrupt while your partner shares their story.
5. Change speakers when I signal. I will also signal when time is up.
6. Are there any questions before we begin? *(Pause to answer questions.)*

7. The first speaker's time begins now. *(Signal at 4 minutes and at 8 minutes, which ends the exercise.)*
8. Now let's form a circle *(or other seating plan)* for faith-sharing questions. *(Continue when all are seated.)*

(Online) *Give the group time to ponder the exercise questions while you assign breakout rooms and time limit. Then give the following instructions.*

Here's how online sharing works:

1. You will be assigned to a breakout room. Click the accept button to get there.
2. Introduce yourself to your partner and decide who speaks first.
3. You each have about four minutes to tell your story with the statement stems.
4. Listening is an important part of being a participant, so please don't interrupt while your partner shares their story.
5. A prompt will appear a minute before you automatically return here to the main room for faith-sharing instructions.
6. I will now send you to your breakout rooms. *(Provide access. Continue when all group members have returned to the main room.)*

3. Faith Sharing (35 minutes)

Script

Before we begin the faith-sharing segment, let's review the Guide to Group Etiquette found in the *Journal*, page 52. *(Review the guide.)* Does anyone have questions?

(Online) *If needed, assign subgroups and time limit for faith-sharing breakout rooms. Then provide access. Participants will automatically return to the main room for the Summary.*

Questions on today's theme: For Whom Are You Looking?

1. Like Mary Magdalene after her loss, did you have bouts of weeping, need to do something with your pain, or get confused by what was happening? Explain.
2. When your loved one died, what role did your faith in God have in what you did? Give an example.
3. Did you wonder what happened to the soul of your beloved, or did you somehow know he or she was with the Lord? Explain.

4. Summary (5 minutes)

- Comment on what the group or subgroups accomplished today.
- Show the *Journal's* Guidepost Bible citation and the Soul Work. Encourage everyone to commit to a time each week to connect to the Lord in this way.
- Announce the next session: Path to Understanding: *Our Source of Consolation.*
- Pray the Prayer to the Giver of Hope (group listens and prays silently):

  O loving God,
  spirit of consolation and giver of hope,
  we thank you for the gift of your faithful people who join us today.
  We ask you to bless and keep them in your care.
  Let us also pray for the souls of our departed loved ones.
  (Pause so that group members may call these to mind.)
  May perpetual light shine upon them and bring eternal rest.
  We ask this through Christ our Lord.
  Amen. *(Make the Sign of the Cross.)*

- Wish everyone a blessed week.

5. Fellowship Break (On-site 30 minutes)

Schedule as desired: before the session begins, before faith sharing, or as a finale.

Season One

Session 2

Path to Understanding

Theme: Our Source of Consolation

On-site items needed:

- » sign-in materials (name tags, pencils, attendance sheet, and signs)
- » pre-session music/player
- » focal point
- » Bibles
- » tissue boxes

On-site and online item:

- » "My Yoke Is Easy" by John Michael Talbot on *Master Collection V.I: The Quiet Side* (CD #2) (optional)

1. Opening (20 minutes)

- Welcome the group to Session 2: Path to Understanding: *Our Source of Consolation.*
- **(On-site)** Thank those who brought refreshments.
- Begin the session with the Sign of the Cross.
    - ⁎ **(On-site)** Pray together the Seasons of Hope Prayer on the back cover of the *Journal.*
    - ⁎ **(Online)** A team member offers the Seasons of Hope Prayer aloud while the group joins in silently.
- Invite participants to state their name and that of the deceased, their relationship, and when the loss occurred. Give an example: "My name is (Donna), and I lost (Erynne), my (daughter), (several months) ago."
- Ask for God-wink stories from the week or insights from the Soul Work.
- Invite sharing of favorite faith or grief-related items.

2. Activity (20 minutes)

Script

For some, the path of mourning is a lonely journey. Many of us are expected to return to "normal" shortly after the loss of our loved one. We soon discover, however, that grief lingers and that healing has its own timetable. Our funeral rites tell us that God is with us in the midst of our suffering. Later, when the visible support of family and friends tapers off, it helps to remember that the love and consolation of Christ remain within our reach.

Let's turn now to **Matthew 11:28–30**. *(Have a teammate read the passage aloud while participants read along in their Bibles.)*

Jesus's words are worth pondering. He invites us to draw near to him as a way of coping with our burdens, but he never intrudes. We must go to him.

(Proceed with the music meditation and writing exercise or do only the exercise.)

Script (music meditation)

Begin playing "My Yoke Is Easy." **(Online)** *Use Share Screen.*
So let's go to him now. Sit back, close your eyes, and settle in your mind an image of the Lord.

Or focus your eyes on the Jesus image on display or a prayer card. Imagine that the voice of the singer belongs to Jesus.

Exercise

(**On-site**) Provide pencils.

Script

Let's open the *Journal* to Marking the Route for session 2.

1. Approach Jesus through the written word by making a list of three things that make you weary during mourning.
2. Then jot down an example of a time when you sought and received Jesus's help with one of those burdens.

I'll signal when it's time to begin faith sharing.

(Online) *If needed, assign faith-sharing breakout rooms and time limit during exercise. Provide room access after you signal. Participants will automatically return to the main room for the Summary.*

3. Faith Sharing (35 minutes)

Questions on today's theme: Our Source of Consolation

1. How did God lighten your burden around the time your loved one passed on? Explain. If no example comes to mind, for what help were you praying?
2. How has God eased your grief recently? Explain.
3. In what way, if any, is your burden lightened by scripture passages or sacred music?

4. Summary (5 minutes)

- Comment on what the group or subgroups accomplished today.
- Announce the next session: Obstacles on the Journey: *Shattered Dreams.*
- Encourage everyone to do the session's Soul Work in the *Journal* this week.
- Pray the Prayer to the Giver of Hope (group listens and prays silently):

  O loving God,
  spirit of consolation and giver of hope,
  we thank you for the gift of your faithful people who join us today.
  We ask you to bless and keep them in your care.
  Let us also pray for the souls of our departed loved ones.
  (Pause so that group members may call these to mind.)
  May perpetual light shine upon them and bring eternal rest.
  We ask this through Christ our Lord.
  Amen. *(Make the Sign of the Cross.)*

- Wish everyone a blessed week.

5. Fellowship Break (On-site 30 minutes)

Schedule as desired: before the session begins, before faith sharing, or as a finale.

Season One

Session 3

Obstacles on the Journey

Theme: Shattered Dreams

On-site items needed:

» sign-in materials
» pre-session music/player
» focal point
» Bibles
» tissue boxes
» pencils

On-site and online item:

» "Abba! Father!" by Carey Landry on *Abba, Father: Prayer Songs of Rev. Carey Landry* (CD) (optional)

1. Opening (20 minutes)

- Welcome the group to Session 3: Obstacles on the Journey: *Shattered Dreams*.
- **(On-site)** Thank those who brought refreshments.
- Begin the session with the Sign of the Cross.
  - ⁎ **(On-site)** Pray the Seasons of Hope Prayer together.
  - ⁎ **(Online)** A team member offers the Seasons of Hope Prayer aloud while the group joins in silently.
- **(On-site)** Explain the purpose of the Network Directory in the *Journal.*
- Ask for God-wink stories from the week or insights from the Soul Work.
- Invite sharing of favorite faith or grief-related items.

2. Activity (15 minutes)

Script

Most of us don't understand what life without our loved one will be like before he or she dies. We learn quickly, though. It might sink in at the moment of death or when the unthinkable message is delivered. Sometimes we become numb to what is happening, which cushions the time around the funeral so that we aren't paralyzed by grief. But eventually we realize that our hopes and dreams of a future with the deceased are gone—shattered like a precious piece of pottery that falls from its shelf.

Let's turn to **Jeremiah 18:1–6.** This prophetic passage from the Old Testament portrays God as the greatest of potters. *(Have a teammate read the passage aloud while participants read along in their Bibles.)*

It's hard to imagine being a pliable clump of clay that God keeps molding into whatever he pleases. Does he want to form us anew as we face our shattered dreams? We'll consider that possibility for the next few minutes.

(Proceed with the music meditation and writing exercise or do only the exercise.)

Script (music meditation)

Begin playing "Abba! Father!" **(Online)** *Use Share Screen.*
While you listen to the music, place yourself in the hands of the Father.

Exercise

(**On-site**) Provide pencils.

Script

Let's open the *Journal* to Marking the Route for session 3.

1. Think about a dream that you had for your loved one that never came to be and left you in need of the healing touch of the Lord.
2. How might you honor that dream in the future?
3. If you want to, jot down your thoughts.

I will signal when it's time to begin faith sharing.

(Online) *If needed, assign faith-sharing breakout rooms and time limit during exercise. Provide access after the signal. Participants will automatically return to the main room for the Summary.*

3. Faith Sharing (40 minutes)

Script

We often forget that even our Lord Jesus had dreams that were shattered during his time among his people.

Questions on today's theme: Shattered Dreams

1. What shattered dream that you had for your loved one would you like to share with us? And how might you honor that dream now?
2. What dream did your loved one have that was fulfilled in their lifetime? Tell us about it.
3. Does it seem as though God is spiritually molding you into something new since your loss? Give an example.

4. Summary (5 minutes)

- Comment on what the group or subgroups accomplished today.
- Announce the next session: Path to Inner Healing: *Finding Joy*.
- Encourage everyone to do the session's Soul Work in the *Journal* this week.
- Pray the Prayer to the Giver of Hope (group listens and prays silently):

> O loving God,
> spirit of consolation and giver of hope,
> we thank you for the gift of your faithful people who join us today.
> We ask you to bless and keep them in your care.
> Let us also pray for the souls of our departed loved ones.
> *(Pause so that group members may call these to mind.)*
> May perpetual light shine upon them and bring eternal rest.
> We ask this through Christ our Lord.
> Amen. *(Make the Sign of the Cross.)*

- Wish everyone a blessed week.

5. Fellowship Break (On-site 30 minutes)

Schedule as desired: before the session begins, before faith sharing, or as a finale.

Season One

Session 4

Path to Inner Healing

Theme: Finding Joy

On-site items needed:

- » sign-in materials
- » pre-session music/player
- » focal point
- » Bibles
- » tissue boxes

1. Opening (20 minutes)

- Welcome the group to Session 4: Path to Inner Healing: *Finding Joy*.
- **(On-site)** Thank those who brought refreshments.
- Begin the session with the Sign of the Cross.
    - ⁕ **(On-site)** Pray the Seasons of Hope Prayer together.
    - ⁕ **(Online)** A team member offers the Seasons of Hope Prayer aloud while group joins in silently.
- Ask for God-wink stories from the week or insights from the Soul Work.
- Invite sharing of favorite faith or grief-related items.

2. Activity (20 minutes)

Script

Have you wondered whether joy will ever be yours again? It's a concern that often goes unspoken during mourning. Yes, life goes on, but you may feel half alive. Things that once made you happy may no longer bring a smile. You may feel empty. Maybe the future seems bleak. Then one day your pain is forgotten for a moment. The relief brings you hope, but when does grief become joy? Our Lord addressed this very concern with his followers when his time with them was almost over. Let's turn to **John 16:19–24** for the story. *(Have a teammate read the passage aloud while participants read along in their Bibles.)*

The Lord's words convey confidence that your grief will become joy. Our next exercise helps you think about that.

Exercise

(**On-site**) Provide pencils.

Let's open the *Journal* to Marking the Route for session 4.

1. Consider what might help you find joy again, especially those things that haven't found a place in your prayers.
2. Then write a letter to God in the space provided. Ask for whatever would rekindle your joy.

I will signal when it's time to begin faith sharing.

(Online) *If needed, assign faith-sharing breakout rooms and time limit during exercise. Provide access after the signal. Participants will automatically return to the main room for the Summary.*

3. Faith Sharing (40 minutes)

Script

The joy that Jesus speaks of in John's gospel tells us to hope and trust in God's benevolence even when we are distressed by the uncertainty of the future. To do so brings everlasting joy of the soul. Our challenge is to hope and trust.

Questions on today's theme: Finding Joy

1. What is the hardest part of the day since your loss? What helps you through it?
2. When a social gathering that once brought joy comes up, do you decline or attend? Does your decision include hope and trust in God? Explain.
3. Has a ritual of faith that honors the memory of your loved one brought you or others a moment of joy? Explain.

SEASON One

4. Summary (5 minutes)

- Comment on what the group or subgroups accomplished today.
- Announce the next session: Way of Suffering: *The Way of the Cross.*
- Encourage everyone to do the session's Soul Work in the *Journal* during the week.
- Pray the Prayer to the Giver of Hope (group listens and prays silently):

  O loving God,
  spirit of consolation and giver of hope,
  we thank you for the gift of your faithful people who join us today.
  We ask you to bless and keep them in your care.
  Let us also pray for the souls of our departed loved ones.
  (Pause so that group members may call these to mind.)
  May perpetual light shine upon them and bring eternal rest.
  We ask this through Christ our Lord.
  Amen. *(Make the Sign of the Cross.)*

- Wish everyone a blessed week.

5. Fellowship Break (On-site 30 minutes)

Schedule as desired: before the session begins, before faith sharing, or as a finale.

Season One

Session 5

Way of Suffering

Theme: The Way of the Cross

On-site items needed:

» sign-in materials
» pre-session music/player
» focal point
» Bibles
» tissue boxes
» Stations of the Cross or illustrated pamphlet
» *Maundy Thursday: Gregorian Chant* (CD) by the Monastic Choir of St. Peter Abbey of Solesmes or *Requiem* (CD) by the Priestly Fraternity of St. Peter (optional)

Online item needed:

» Stations of the Cross images

1. Opening (20 minutes)

- Welcome the group to Session 5: Way of Suffering: *The Way of the Cross*.
- **(On-site)** Thank those who brought refreshments.
- Begin the session with the Sign of the Cross.
  - **(On-site)** Pray the Seasons of Hope Prayer together.
  - **(Online)** A team member offers the Seasons of Hope Prayer aloud while the group joins in silently.
- Ask for God-wink stories from the week or insights from the Soul Work.
- Invite sharing of favorite faith or grief-related items.

2. Activity (20 minutes)

SEASON One

Script

If you wonder whether God understands our pain, consider what Jesus went through on the way to Calvary. The brutality he endured went far beyond the physical. Surely, his spirit suffered a beating that those who mourn can recognize.

Let's turn to **Luke 23:13–56** to focus on what the Lord went through. *(Have a teammate read the passage aloud while participants read along in their Bibles.)*

The Stations of the Cross capture the Passion of Christ in pictures for us. This ancient tradition is a powerful way to pray and grow closer to the Lord in spirit. It opens our heart to his love and consolation.

(Select Maundy Thursday *or* Requiem *and the exercise or do only the exercise.)*

Exercise

(On-site) Provide pencils. Show Stations of the Cross by pictures, a visit to a church, or a pamphlet you distribute. The *Journal* lists the fourteen stations.
(Online) Offer images of the Stations of the Cross and music using Share Screen.

Script

Let's open the *Journal* to Marking the Route for session 5.

1. For the next few minutes, contemplate the Passion of Christ by viewing the Stations of the Cross as though you were there among the crowd.
2. Identify which station shows the kind of suffering or sorrow you currently experience.
3. Jot down your thoughts.

I will signal when it's time to begin faith sharing.

(Online) *If needed, assign faith-sharing breakout rooms and time limit during writing exercise. Provide access after the signal. Participants will automatically return to the main room for the Summary.*

3. Faith Sharing (45 minutes)

Questions on today's theme: The Way of the Cross

1. Which station reminds you of your grief? Tell us why.
2. In what way have others helped you carry your cross of grieving? Did you have to ask for assistance, or was it an unanticipated gift?

3. How do you reach out now to others who face suffering and sorrow? Are you a Simon, Veronica, weeping person, disciple at the Cross, or silent bystander? Explain.

4. Summary (5 minutes)

- Comment on what the group or subgroups accomplished today.
- Announce the season's last session: Final Destination: *Untie Him.*
- Ask participants to bring a framed photo of their loved one to the last session.
- Encourage everyone to do the session's Soul Work in the *Journal* during the week.
- Pray the Prayer to the Giver of Hope (group listens and prays silently):

  O loving God,
  spirit of consolation and giver of hope,
  we thank you for the gift of your faithful people who join us today.
  We ask you to bless and keep them in your care.
  Let us also pray for the souls of our departed loved ones.
  (Pause so that group members may call these to mind.)
  May perpetual light shine upon them and bring eternal rest.
  We ask this through Christ our Lord.
  Amen. *(Make the Sign of the Cross.)*

- Wish everyone a blessed week.

5. Fellowship Break (On-site 30 minutes)

Schedule as desired: before the session begins, before faith sharing, or as a finale.

Season One

Session 6

Final Destination

Theme: Untie Him

On-site items needed:

» sign-in materials
» pre-session music/player
» focal point and table large enough for framed pictures
» chairs formed in a circle that includes the focal point table
» Bibles
» tissue boxes
» pencils

On-site and online items:

» camera (optional)
» Season Survey

1. Opening (10 minutes)

- Welcome the group to Session 6: Final Destination: *Untie Him*.
- **(On-site)** Thank those who brought refreshments.
- Begin the session with the Sign of the Cross.
    - **(On-site)** Pray the Seasons of Hope Prayer together.
    - **(Online)** A team member offers the Seasons of Hope Prayer aloud while the group joins in silently.
- **(On-site)** Ask all to join in a group photo (optional).
- **(Online)** Ask all to smile for a group photo on screen (optional).
- Use the script below for sharing of favorite pictures of loved ones.

2. Activity (30 minutes)

Exercise

Script

Each week in session we have honored our deceased loved ones with word and prayer. Today we go a step further. You will each have a chance to:

1. Introduce your loved one in the picture you brought and tell why the photo or setting is a favorite of yours.
2. **(On-site)** Then bring the item to the table with our image of Jesus. This brief walk is a symbol of your journey with us these past weeks.

Who would like to go first? *(Continue after everyone has shared.)*

Thank you for sharing. It's nice to know more about your loved ones. Now it's time for our scripture story.

Scripture

Script

We go on living after our losses, but down deep we may still yearn for our loved ones. Certain events, the holidays, or places that remind us of the past may bring pain. People say the hurt eventually diminishes, but we may wonder if we'll ever feel whole again. When we seek Christ in the midst of sorrow, the scriptures can be great teachers.

Let's turn to **John 11:1–44** to see how Jesus and his friends faced the death of Lazarus. *(Have a teammate read the passage aloud while participants read along in their Bibles.)*

Now let's apply the story through faith sharing.

(Online) *If needed, assign subgroups and time limit for faith-sharing breakout rooms. Then provide access. Participants will automatically return to the main room for the Summary.*

3. Faith Sharing (40 minutes)

Questions on today's theme: Untie Him

1. In what way, if any, does the scripture passage remind you of your faith in the midst of losing your loved one? Give an example.
2. Around the time your loved one died, how did the Lord respond to your call for help? Explain.

3. Do any ties with your loved one need to be untied? Explain.

4. Summary (15 minutes)

SEASON One

- Comment on group accomplishments this season.
- Share future Seasons of Hope offerings and ask participants to spread the word.
- Encourage everyone to do the Soul Work this week.
- **(On-site)** Have participants complete and submit the *Journal's* Season Survey.
    - **(Online)** Have participants complete and return the Season Survey emailed to them for this purpose.
- Pray the Prayer to the Giver of Hope *(ask everyone to pray silently but to say the name of their beloved aloud during the pause)*:

  O loving God,
  spirit of consolation and giver of hope,
  we thank you for the gift of your faithful people who join us today.
  We ask you to bless and keep them in your care.
  Let us also pray for the souls of our departed loved ones.
  (Name your beloved and pause while others name theirs.)
  May perpetual light shine upon them and bring eternal rest.
  We ask this through Christ our Lord.
  Amen. *(Make the Sign of the Cross.)*

- Wish everyone well.

5. Fellowship Break (On-site 30 minutes)

Schedule as desired: before the session begins, before faith sharing, or as a finale.

Season Two

Session 1

Point of Departure

Theme: Remembering

On-site items needed:

» sign-in materials (name tags, markers, attendance sheet, and signs)
» Season Two *Journals* for group
» pre-session music/player
» focal point (image of Jesus)
» Bibles
» tissue boxes
» timer or watch
» bell (optional)
» refreshment sign-up sheet (optional)

1. Opening (20 minutes)

- On behalf of the team, welcome the group to Session 1: Point of Departure: *Remembering.*
- Begin the session with the Sign of the Cross.
    - **(On-site)** Pray together the Seasons of Hope Prayer on the back cover of the *Journal.*
    - **(Online)** A team member offers the Seasons of Hope Prayer aloud while the group joins in silently.
- Keep introductions brief. Invite participants to say their name and relation to their deceased loved one. Give an example: "My name is (Mary), and I lost my (husband)."

Assure them that they will share more during the session.

- Use the script below to explain the Seasons of Hope program, *Journals*, and any housekeeping details.

Script

"Blessed are those who mourn," our Lord assured us, "for they will be comforted" (Mt 5:4). Seasons of Hope brings us together to share in God's love. The support of this community will enable you to give voice to your unique journey and take a step toward healing and spiritual growth.

You are an expert on your grief. We aren't here to teach you about its stages. You meet them on your journey. Instead, we will explore mourning through scripture, prayer, reflection, and faith sharing. We will help you focus on your relationship with the Lord and the many ways his Church offers consolation. Along the way, you will find Jesus in others who mourn and within your own heart.

We use the Bible each week. The *Journal's* Guidepost page has the Bible citation of the passage you read here and again at home. **(On-site)** Does anyone need to borrow a Bible? *(Have a teammate provide them.)*

Please have your *Journal* handy too. We use it for our opening exercise in group and for Soul Work at home after each session. The Soul Work gives a fresh perspective on the scripture reading. Plus, it allows you to reflect on your relationship with the Lord, write about your loss, and share in a consoling tradition of the Church.

The group session officially concludes with the Summary, which sends you forth with the Prayer to the Giver of Hope.

Now for some housekeeping details:

- We start promptly each week, so please arrive a few minutes early.
- If you can't make a session, please tell us.
- Please silence your cell phone.
- **(Online)** Please mute your speaker if your room gets noisy.
- **(On-site)** Restrooms are located in the . . .
- Each session you are invited to show one of your favorite faith or grief-related items. It could be a book, poem, prayer, song, website, devotional item, etc.
- **(On-site)** The fellowship break is at *(indicate time)*. It's our informal time to share refreshments and get to know each other as neighbors and community members.
- (**On-site** optional) We need help with refreshments. Please sign up to bring one plate of snacks sometime this season. Thank you. This week *(give names)* brought snacks. Let's offer our thanks with a round of applause.

Does anyone have questions?

2. Activity (20 minutes)

Script

The Lord taught about his death and resurrection before they happened. Nevertheless, the empty tomb came as a shock to his followers—both women and men. The scriptures reveal a variety of reactions that parallel what many of us experience when someone we love dies. Let's turn to **Luke 24:1–12**. *(Have a teammate read the passage aloud while participants read along in their Bibles.)*

The women who encountered the empty tomb of Christ had a profound story to tell. Unfailing faith in the Lord allowed them to accept that he was alive. The apostles didn't believe the women; in fact, Peter had to investigate the tomb himself. How fortunate we are that these disciples responded differently. It encourages us to embrace the unique reactions people have to losing a loved one.

The way you and I respond to loss stems, in part, from the way our family of origin reacted to death. Today's activity helps us connect our past to our present loss. Let's open the *Journal* to Marking the Route for session 1.

Exercise

Script

With a partner, you will focus on your first experience with wakes and funerals by completing these statements:

- My name is ________________________.
- The first family member whose death I recall was my _____________, who died when I was _____ years old.
- What I remember most about wakes and funerals when I was a child is . . .
- The thing my parent(s) did that most impressed me is . . .
- The part God played in what I remember is . . .

(On-site) Here's how sharing works:

1. Find a partner—preferably someone you don't know well. *(Continue when pairs are formed.)*
2. Decide who speaks first.
3. You each have about four minutes to tell your story with the statement stems.
4. Listening is an important part of being a participant, so please don't interrupt while your partner shares their story.
5. Change speakers when I signal. I will also signal when time is up.
6. Are there any questions before we begin? *(Pause to answer questions.)*

7. The first speaker's time begins now. *(Signal at 4 minutes and 8 minutes, which ends the exercise.)*
8. Now let's form a circle *(or other seating plan)* for faith-sharing questions. (*Continue when all are seated.)*

(Online) *Give the group time to ponder the exercise questions while you assign breakout rooms and time limit. Then give the following instructions.*

Here's how online sharing works:

1. You will be sent to a breakout room. Click the accept button to get there.
2. Introduce yourself to your partner and decide who speaks first.
3. You each have about four minutes to tell your story with the statement stems.
4. Listening is an important part of being a participant, so please don't interrupt while your partner shares their story.
5. A prompt will appear a minute before you automatically return to the main room.
6. I will now send you to your breakout rooms. *(Provide access. Continue when all group members have returned to the main room.)*

3. Faith Sharing (35 minutes)

Script

Before we begin the faith-sharing segment, let's review the Guide to Group Etiquette found in the *Journal*, page 52. *(Review the guide.)* Does anyone have questions?

(Online) *If needed, assign subgroups and time limit for faith-sharing breakout rooms. Then provide access. Participants will automatically return to the main room for the Summary.*

Questions on today's theme: Remembering

1. Like the women at the tomb, did you have moments of disbelief, fear, wonder, relief, or something else after your loss? What comfort, if any, did faith bring to those moments?
2. Does a visit to the grave or another place of interment help your grieving? Explain.
3. Since your loss, have you grown closer to the Lord, or has practicing the faith become a challenge? Give an example.

4. Summary (5 minutes)

- Comment on what the group or subgroups accomplished today.
- Show the *Journal's* Guidepost Bible citation and the Soul Work. Encourage everyone to commit to a time each week to connect to the Lord in this way.

- Announce the next session: Path to Understanding: *Seeking Consolation*.
- Pray the Prayer to the Giver of Hope (group listens and prays silently):

  O loving God,
  spirit of consolation and giver of hope,
  we thank you for the gift of your faithful people who join us today.
  We ask you to bless and keep them in your care.
  Let us also pray for the souls of our departed loved ones.
  (Pause so that group members may call these to mind.)
  May perpetual light shine upon them and bring eternal rest.
  We ask this through Christ our Lord.
  Amen. *(Make the Sign of the Cross.)*

- Wish everyone a blessed week.

5. Fellowship Break (On-site 30 minutes)

Schedule as desired: before the session begins, before faith sharing, or as a finale.

Season Two

Session 2

Path to Understanding

Theme: Seeking Consolation

On-site items needed:

» sign-in materials (name tags, markers, attendance sheet, and signs)
» pre-session music/player
» focal point
» Bibles
» tissue boxes
» pencils

On-site and online item:

» "Sacred Silence" by Tom Booth on *Unravel* (CD) or "Song over the Water" by Marty Haugen on *Anthology II: 1985–1989* (CD) (optional)

1. Opening (20 minutes)

- Welcome the group to Session 2: Path to Understanding: *Seeking Consolation.*
- **(On-site)** Thank those who brought refreshments.
- Begin the session with the Sign of the Cross.
  - **(On-site)** Pray the Seasons of Hope Prayer together.
  - **(Online)** A team member offers the Seasons of Hope Prayer aloud while the group joins in silently.
- Invite participants to state their name and that of the deceased, their relationship, and when the loss occurred. Give an example: "My name is (Mary), and I lost (Joe), my (husband), (a year) ago."
- Ask for God-wink stories from the week or insights from the Soul Work.

- Invite sharing of favorite faith or grief-related items.

2. Activity (20 minutes)

Script

Moving forward with life after losing a loved one sometimes seems impossible. Grieving may leave us with a defeated attitude that can cripple the spirit. This is especially true if we withdraw from familiar people and activities that remind us of our loss. We may learn not to speak of our grief because others don't seem to understand. We may grieve alone even though well-meaning people surround us.

The truth is, we are never truly alone. Jesus understands suffering and wants to console us. In today's scripture, we witness his desire to heal a crippled man who can't seem to move on. Let's turn to **John 5:1–9.** (*Have a teammate read the passage aloud while participants read along in their Bibles.)*

The passage reveals much about Jesus. He knows who is hurting. He seeks the person's wishes. His question about a cure must have seemed odd to the man since the water of the nearby pool was believed to have healing power.

We believe that water is a symbol of birth and rebirth, and Jesus is the "living water" (Jn 4:10). Today's passage reveals that on Jesus's word alone the crippled man was healed. The question for us is simple: do we want to be healed by Christ and move on with our lives?

(Proceed with the music meditation and writing exercise or do only the exercise.)

Script (music meditation)

Begin playing "Sacred Silence" *or* "Song over the Water." **(Online)** *Use Share Screen.*

Let's go to him now. Sit back, close your eyes, and listen to the music as you bring an image of the Lord to mind. Imagine his healing water flowing over you, washing away your sorrow and tears.

(Proceed to exercise when song is over.)

Exercise

(On-site) Provide pencils.

Script

Another powerful way to approach Jesus is through the written word. Open the *Journal* to Marking the Route for session 2. Take the next few minutes to:

1. Write to him about what seems to cripple you spiritually.
2. Let Jesus know whether you are ready to pick up the pieces of your life.

I will signal when it's time to begin faith sharing.

(Online) *If needed, assign faith sharing breakout rooms and time limit during writing exercise. Provide access after the signal. Participants will automatically return to the main room for the Summary.*

3. Faith Sharing (35 minutes)

Script

Jesus asked the paralyzed person, "Do you want to be well?" His question gets to the heart of mourning, too.

Questions on today's theme: Seeking Consolation

1. Have you noticed the Lord (or others) nudging you to "pick up your mat"? Give an example or tell us what part of grieving paralyzes you.
2. How do you feel about moving forward? Explain.
3. What needs to be reborn in your spiritual life now? Explain.

4. Summary (5 minutes)

- Comment on what the group or subgroups accomplished today.
- Encourage everyone to do the session's Soul Work in the *Journal* this week.
- Announce the next session: Obstacles on the Journey: *Stumbling Blocks.*
- **(Online)** Ask everyone to bring a stone to the next session that symbolizes their stumbling block to healing.
- Pray the Prayer to the Giver of Hope (group listens and prays silently*)*:

  O loving God,
  spirit of consolation and giver of hope,
  we thank you for the gift of your faithful people who join us today.
  We ask you to bless and keep them in your care.
  Let us also pray for the souls of our departed loved ones.
  (Pause so that group members may call these to mind.)
  May perpetual light shine upon them and bring eternal rest.
  We ask this through Christ our Lord.
  Amen. *(Make the Sign of the Cross.)*

- Wish everyone a blessed week.

5. Fellowship Break (On-site 30 minutes)

Schedule as desired: before the session begins, before faith sharing, or as a finale.

Season Two

Session 3

Obstacles on the Journey

Theme: Stumbling Blocks

On-site items needed:

» sign-in materials
» pre-session music/player
» focal point
» Bibles
» tissue boxes
» pencils
» small basket with stones of various sizes, shapes, colors, and textures

Online items needed:

» stones brought by group members or digital images of stones

1. Opening (20 minutes)

- Welcome the group to Session 3: Obstacles on the Journey: *Stumbling Blocks*.
- **(On-site)** Thank those who brought refreshments.
- Begin the session with the Sign of the Cross.
  - **(On-site)** Pray the Seasons of Hope Prayer together.
  - **(Online)** A team member offers the Seasons of Hope Prayer aloud while the group joins in silently.
- **(On-site)** Explain the purpose of the Network Directory in the *Journal*.
- Ask for God-wink stories from the week or insights from the Soul Work.
- Invite sharing of favorite faith or grief-related items.

2. Activity (20 minutes)

Script

When we lose a loved one, the change of seasons, holidays, or other reminders of the dearly departed can make us feel sad. Yet we know through the writings of the prophets of the Old Testament that God yearns to revive the hearts of those crushed in spirit. Let's turn to **Isaiah 57:14–15** to hear words of consolation. *(Have a teammate read the passage aloud while participants read along in their Bibles.)*

The passage speaks of God's loving concern for those who suffer a major loss in life. It says the obstacles (stumbling blocks) before us will be removed because we are God's people. We are meant to build up God's kingdom. We can use our stumbling blocks as a bridge that brings us closer to God. When our grief is used for good, it gains meaning for us as well as other believers. So the question for each of us becomes, "Could it be that a crushed spirit is a pathway for us to grow spiritually?"

Exercise

(On-site) Provide pencils and a basket of stones.

Script

For this activity you need a stone that has the size, color, shape, or texture that represents the stumbling block you currently face on your journey through mourning.

(On-site) Select one from the basket that is being passed around.

(Online) Take out the stone you found for this session. If you need one, imagine one you'd select at the beach or use the images on the screen *(offer via Share Screen).*

(Continue once everyone has a real or virtual stone.)

Open the *Journal* to Marking the Route for session 3.

1. For the next few minutes, write to Jesus and explain to him what the size, color, shape, and texture of the stone you selected tells you about your loss.
2. Then describe the details of your "real" stumbling block and ask for his help with it.

I will signal when it's time to begin faith sharing.

(Online) *If needed, assign faith-sharing breakout rooms and time limit during the writing exercise. Provide access after the signal. Participants will automatically return to the main room for the Summary.*

3. Faith Sharing (40 minutes)

Questions on today's theme: Stumbling Blocks

1. Why does your stone's size, color, shape, or texture remind you of a stumbling block? Show the stone to us and explain.
2. Do certain things make you stumble or take a step backward as you mourn? Give an example.
3. What other stone on your path to healing needs a nudge, patience, or a miracle?

4. Summary (5 minutes)

- Comment on what the group or subgroups accomplished today.
- Announce the next session: Path to Inner Healing: *Living Hope.*
- Encourage everyone to do the session's Soul Work in the *Journal* this week.
- Pray the Prayer to the Giver of Hope (group listens and prays silently):

  O loving God,
  spirit of consolation and giver of hope,
  we thank you for the gift of your faithful people who join us today.
  We ask you to bless and keep them in your care.
  Let us also pray for the souls of our departed loved ones.
  (Pause so that group members may call these to mind.)
  May perpetual light shine upon them and bring eternal rest.
  We ask this through Christ our Lord.
  Amen. *(Make the Sign of the Cross.)*

- Wish everyone a blessed week.

5. Fellowship Break (On-site 30 minutes)

Schedule as desired: before the session begins, before faith sharing, or as a finale.

Season Two

Session 4

Path to Inner Healing

Theme: Living Hope

On-site items needed:

» sign-in materials
» pre-session music/player
» focal point
» Bibles
» tissue boxes
» colored paper and markers
» glass bowl and water

Online item needed:

» "Pachelbel's Canon" by Daniel Kobialka on *Timeless Motion* (CD)

1. Opening (20 minutes)

- Welcome the group to Session 4: Path to Inner Healing: *Living Hope*.
- **(On-site)** Thank those who brought refreshments.
- Begin the session with the Sign of the Cross.
    - **(On-site)** Pray the Seasons of Hope Prayer together.
    - **(Online)** A team member offers the Seasons of Hope Prayer aloud while the group joins in silently.
- Ask for God-wink stories from the week or insights from the Soul Work.
- Invite sharing of favorite faith or grief-related items.

2. Activity (20 minutes)

Script

The greatest treasure we can possess is faith in God. The scripture of this session affirms what the faithful know firsthand—that faith is subject to trials that test our belief in God. In the throes of grief, recognizing God's loving presence brings hope.

Let's turn to **1 Peter 1:3–9.** *(Have a teammate read the passage aloud while participants read along in their Bibles.)*

Scripture reminds us that our hope stems from the Resurrection of our Lord. Hope in salvation is his gift to us—a gift that is present even when losing a loved one leaves us downcast about the trials we face.

(Proceed with either the on-site or online version of Part 1 of today's exercise)

SEASON **Two**

On-site Exercise (Provide colored paper and markers)

Part 1.

Script

Grieving colors our lives. This week's group exercise gives us one way to take charge today, instead of letting grief rule us.

1. Select a shade of colored paper that symbolizes your grief. There is no correct color, just one that appeals to your imagination.
2. Label the paper "My Grief."
3. If you like, name a specific trial on the paper or draw about it.
4. Then take your grief paper and make it smaller. Tear it, fold it, or crumple it. Show your "grief" what you'd like to do with it.
   (Pause while participants complete the process.)
5. Now hand your grief over to the Lord. One by one come to the prayer table and place what remains of your "grief" in the bowl of water that symbolizes Jesus's healing power.
   (Pause until everyone finishes. Then proceed to the Exercise for Part 2.)

Online Exercise (Read guided imagery Script to group)

Part 1.

Script

We'll use our faith and some guided imagery to encounter God's loving presence and the hope God longs to give us on the path to inner healing. I'll go slowly and pause every so often so that you can experience the sensations the images bring.

Let's begin:

Get comfortable in your chair.

Let peace gently flow over you.

Now close your eyes . . . and take a deep breath and let the breath out slowly.

Breathe in . . . Breathe out . . . In . . . Out . . . In . . . Out . . . In . . . Out.

Relax . . . Be calm.

Remember that the love of God surrounds you.

Now go into the stillness of your mind and find a wide, deserted beach . . .

Listen to the cry of seagulls . . . and the roar of surf pounding the shore.

See the mist spray into the air . . .

Let the chilly wind nip at you . . .

Taste the salt it leaves on your lips . . .

It tastes like your tears . . . the ones that brought you to this lonely beach with its sad gray sky . . .

See yourself walking slowly . . . staring down at lifeless sand . . . shoulders stooped by the loss of your beloved . . .

Think of the struggles you face . . . Think about how life has turned upside down.

You wander along head down, lost in thought. . .

Now look up. You see the beach is no longer deserted.

A man is headed toward you.

He looks like Jesus . . . Yes, it *is* Jesus! . . . He reaches out to you, arms wide open.

Go to him now.

Run, run if you want to . . . Don't let the pounding of your heart stop you.

Don't be afraid . . . Let yourself hug him . . .

. . . and let Jesus hug away your pain . . . your sadness . . .

Now walk arm in arm with him and tell him your concerns.

Let them pour out of you . . . whatever weighs you down the most . . .

Ask Jesus what you need to do to find inner peace.

Jesus stops to face you. He says, "Show me what's in your pocket."

You wonder: *Is* there anything in my pocket? . . . But when you reach in, you find a stone.

You offer it to Jesus.

He smiles and takes it from your trembling hand.

Listen as he says:

"Let this stone be a symbol of your grief . . . Surely, your pain is bigger than this. You are as strong as stone. And you have courage too!

"Grief will not destroy you . . . No, it draws you close to me."

"In time, you'll be healed . . . for you have faith and hope in me!"

"Do not be afraid. I am with you always. My peace I give you."

Let his peace wash over you . . .

Be comforted by it. Cling to it . . .

Breathe in . . . Breathe out . . . Breathe in . . . Breathe out . . .

Slowly come back to this time and session.

When you are ready, open your eyes . . .

Welcome back!

(Stop background music and invite comments on the guided experience. Then proceed to the Exercise (Part 2).

Exercise

Part 2. (On-site) Provide pencils.

Script

Let's open the *Journal* to Marking the Route for session 4.

Take a few minutes to write a note of thanks to Jesus for taking your "grief" from you. I will signal when it's time to begin faith sharing.

(Online) *If needed, assign faith-sharing breakout rooms and time limit during writing exercise. Provide access after the signal. Participants will automatically return to the main room for the Summary.*

3. Faith Sharing (45 minutes)

Script

God's loving presence brings hope during mourning. Let's look at some sources of hope that are close to home.

Questions on today's theme: Living Hope

1. Has someone brought hope into your mourning? Tell us about it.
2. Our Catholic faith has many traditions that inspire hope. Can you share a specific practice you do to help yourself? Has it affected your thoughts about the present? The future?
3. Is there a Church tradition you do with family or friends that brings you hope? If not, is there something else you do with them that brings hope? Explain.

4. Summary (5 minutes)

- Comment on what the group or subgroups accomplished today.
- Announce the next session: Way of Suffering: *The Cross.*
- Ask participants to bring their rosary next week.
- Encourage everyone to do the session's Soul Work this week.
- Pray the Prayer to the Giver of Hope (group listens and prays silently):

  O loving God,
  spirit of consolation and giver of hope,
  we thank you for the gift of your faithful people who join us today.
  We ask you to bless and keep them in your care.
  Let us also pray for the souls of our departed loved ones.
  (Pause so that group members may call these to mind.)
  May perpetual light shine upon them and bring eternal rest.
  We ask this through Christ our Lord.
  Amen. *(Make the Sign of the Cross.)*

- Wish everyone a blessed week.

5. Fellowship Break (On-site 30 minutes)

Schedule as desired: before the session begins, before faith sharing, or as a finale.

Season Two

Session 5

Way of Suffering

Theme: The Cross

On-site items needed:

» sign-in materials
» pre-session music/player
» focal point
» Bibles
» tissue boxes
» rosaries to share if needed
» pencils

On-site and online items needed:

» rosaries brought by group members
» *Mater Eucharistiae* (CD) by the Dominican Sisters of Mary, Mother of the Eucharist, or *Benedicta: Marian Chant from Norcia* by the Monks of Norcia (optional)

1. Opening (15 minutes)

- Welcome the group to Session 5: Way of Suffering: *The Cross*.
- **(On-site)** Thank those who brought refreshments.
- Begin the session with the Sign of the Cross.
    - ⁕ **(On-site)** Pray the Seasons of Hope Prayer together.
    - ⁕ **(Online)** A team member offers the Seasons of Hope Prayer aloud while the group joins in silently.
- Ask for God-wink stories from the week or insights from the Soul Work.
- Invite sharing of favorite faith or grief-related items.

2. Activity (15 minutes)

Script

The faithful who lose a loved one know that suffering is part of discipleship. Let's turn to **Luke 9:22–24** to see what the Gospel teaches. *(Have a teammate read the passage aloud while participants read along in their Bibles.)*

Our losses happen, but Jesus says we have a choice about how we handle them. We can bear our cross alone or share it with the Lord and let him set the pace for us. When he steers us to a Seasons of Hope group, we find consolation on our painful journey. Jesus does warn, however, that the road ahead will be difficult even with him as a guide.

The Church has given us many beautiful traditions of prayer to help us carry our crosses. Many of us rely on the Rosary. Rooted in sacred scripture, it helps us meditate on the lives and suffering of Jesus and Blessed Mother Mary. Prayerful reflection on its mysteries deepens our convictions of faith, soothes our heart, and strengthens our will to follow the Lord (*CCC* 2708).

Today's exercise calls for meditation on the Cross of Christ using the Rosary.

(Proceed with Mater Eucharistiae *or* Benedicta: Marian Chant from Norcia *and the writing exercise or do only the exercise.)*

SEASON Two

Exercise

(On-site) Provide pencils.

Script

Let's open the *Journal* to Marking the Route for session 5. In the next few minutes:

1. Use the crucifix on your rosary to contemplate the Cross of Christ and consider the mystery of his suffering for us.
2. Think about your own cross of sorrow. Has it drawn you closer to the Lord? Does it help you sense that he understands your pain during these difficult times?
3. If you like, jot down your thoughts.

(On-site) Does anyone need a rosary? *(Provide rosaries as needed.)*
I will signal when it's time to begin faith sharing.

(Online) *If needed, assign faith-sharing breakout rooms and time limit during writing exercise. Provide access after the signal. Participants will automatically return to the main room for the Summary.*

3. Faith Sharing (50 minutes)

Script

You bear many different crosses during mourning. Let's look at some examples.

Questions on today's theme: The Cross

1. Which cross keeps you from the Lord? Tell us about it and how you deal with it.
2. Which cross in particular brings you close to the Lord? Explain.
3. Does praying the Rosary or turning to the Blessed Mother help you cope with your grief? If so, share an example.

4. Summary (5 minutes)

- Comment on what the group or subgroups accomplished today.
- Announce the last session of this season: Final Destination: *Do Not Be Afraid.*
- Ask participants to bring an item next week that reminds them of their departed loved one.
- Encourage everyone to do the session's Soul Work this week.
- Pray the Prayer to the Giver of Hope (group listens and prays silently):

  O loving God,
  spirit of consolation and giver of hope,
  we thank you for the gift of your faithful people who join us today.
  We ask you to bless and keep them in your care.
  Let us also pray for the souls of our departed loved ones.
  (Pause so that group members may call these to mind.)
  May perpetual light shine upon them and bring eternal rest.
  We ask this through Christ our Lord.
  Amen. *(Make the Sign of the Cross.)*

- Wish everyone a blessed week.

5. Fellowship Break (On-site 30 minutes)

Schedule as desired: before the session begins, before faith sharing, or as a finale.

Season Two

Session 6

Final Destination

Theme: Do Not Be Afraid

On-site items needed:

» sign-in materials
» pre-session music/player
» focal point table for items brought by group
» chairs formed in a circle that includes the table
» Bibles
» tissue boxes
» pencils
» something that reminds you of your loved one

On-site and online items:

» camera (optional)
» Season Survey

1. Opening (10 minutes)

- Welcome the group to Session 6: Final Destination: *Do Not Be Afraid.*
- **(On-site)** Thank those who brought refreshments.
- Begin the session with the Sign of the Cross.
    - **(On-site)** Pray the Seasons of Hope Prayer together.
    - **(Online)** A team member offers the Seasons of Hope Prayer aloud while the group joins in silently.
- **(On-site)** Ask all to join in a group photo (optional).
- **(Online)** Ask all to smile for a group photo on screen (optional).
- Use the script below for sharing of items related to loved ones.

2. Activity (25 minutes)

Exercise

Script

Each week in session we have honored our deceased loved ones with word and prayer. Today we go a step further. You will each have a chance to:

1. Show us something that reminds you of your loved one and tell why it is special to you.
2. **(On-site)** Then bring the item to the table with our image of Jesus. This brief walk is a symbol of your journey with us these past weeks.

Who would like to go first? *(Continue after everyone has shared their special item.)*

Thank you for sharing. It's nice to know more about your loved ones. Now it's time for our scripture story.

Scripture

Script

It seems that people of faith have a powerful advantage when death occurs. Let's turn to **Luke 8:40–42, 49–56** to learn what scripture has to say on the topic. *(Have a teammate read the passage aloud while participants read along in their Bibles.)*

We can understand why the synagogue official sought Jesus for a dying child. Didn't we seek the Lord's help for our loved ones? We may have hoped for a miracle, but sometimes God wants our loved ones to have eternal rest.

In our grief, it helps to remember that nothing will stop the love of the Lord. The passage relates that Jesus had to work his way through a crowd that crushed in on him, but he rescued the child. Surely, your loved one also received his loving mercy. He is here for you, too.

(Online) *If needed, assign subgroups and time limit for faith-sharing breakout rooms. Then provide access. Participants will automatically return to the main room for the Summary.*

3. Faith Sharing (35 minutes)

Questions on today's theme: Do Not Be Afraid

1. In what way did you invite Jesus into your sorrow so you wouldn't be afraid? Explain.
2. Have any of your beliefs about God changed during mourning? Give an example.
3. What has sharing your faith and grief at Seasons of Hope meant to you?

4. Summary (15 minutes)

- Comment on group accomplishments this season.
- Share future Seasons of Hope offerings and ask participants to spread the word.
- Encourage everyone to do the Soul Work this week.
- **(On-site)** Have participants complete and submit the *Journal's* Season Survey.
    - **(Online)** Have participants complete and return the Season Survey emailed to them for this purpose.
- Pray the Prayer to the Giver of Hope (ask everyone to pray silently but to say the name of their beloved aloud during the pause):

    O loving God,
    spirit of consolation and giver of hope,
    we thank you for the gift of your faithful people who join us today.
    We ask you to bless and keep them in your care.
    Let us also pray for the souls of our departed loved ones.
    (Name your beloved and pause while others name theirs.)
    May perpetual light shine upon them and bring eternal rest.
    We ask this through Christ our Lord.
    Amen. *(Make the Sign of the Cross.)*

- Wish everyone a blessed week.

5. Fellowship Break (On-site 30 minutes)

Schedule as desired: before the session begins, before faith sharing, or as a finale.

Season Three

Session 1

Point of Departure

Theme: Believing

On-site items needed:

» sign-in materials (name tags, markers, attendance sheet, and signs)
» Season Three *Journals* for group
» pre-session music/player
» focal point (image of Jesus)
» Bibles
» tissue boxes
» timer or watch
» bell (optional)
» refreshment sign-up sheet (optional)

1. Opening (20 minutes)

- On behalf of the team, welcome the group to Session 1: Point of Departure: *Believing*.
- Begin the session with the Sign of the Cross.
    - **(On-site)** Pray together the Seasons of Hope Prayer on the back cover of the *Journal*.
    - **(Online)** A team member offers the Seasons of Hope Prayer aloud while the group joins in silently.
- Keep introductions brief. Invite participants to say their name and relation to their deceased loved one. Give an example: "My name is (Jack), and I lost my (wife)." Assure them that they will share more during the session.

- Use the script below to explain the Seasons of Hope program, *Journals*, and any housekeeping details.

Script

"Blessed are those who mourn," our Lord assured us, "for they will be comforted" (Mt 5:4). Seasons of Hope brings us together to share in God's love. The support of this community will enable you to give voice to your unique journey and take a step toward healing and spiritual growth.

You are an expert on your grief. We aren't here to teach you about its stages. You meet them on your journey. Instead, we will explore mourning through scripture, prayer, reflection, and faith sharing. We will help you focus on your relationship with the Lord and the many ways his Church offers consolation. Along the way, you will find Jesus in others who mourn and within your own heart.

We use the Bible each week. The *Journal's* Guidepost page has the Bible citation of the passage you read here and again at home.

(On-site) Does anyone need to borrow a Bible? *(Have a teammate provide them.)*

Please have your *Journal* handy too. We use it for our opening exercise in group and for Soul Work at home after each session. The Soul Work gives a fresh perspective on the scripture reading. Plus, it allows you to reflect on your relationship with the Lord, write about your loss, and share in a consoling tradition of the Church.

The group session officially concludes with the Summary, which sends you forth with the Prayer to the Giver of Hope.

Now for some housekeeping details:

- We start promptly each week, so please arrive a few minutes early.
- If you can't make a session, please tell us.
- Please silence your cell phone.
- **(Online)** Please mute your speaker if your room gets noisy.
- **(On-site)** Restrooms are located in the . . .
- Each session, you are invited to show one of your favorite faith or grief-related items. It could be a book, poem, prayer, song, website, devotional item, etc.
- **(On-site)** The fellowship break is at *(indicate time)*. It's our informal time to share refreshments and get to know each other as neighbors and community members.
- (**On-site** optional) We need help with refreshments. Please sign up to bring one plate of snacks sometime this season. Thank you. This week *(give names)* brought snacks. Let's offer our thanks with a round of applause.

Does anyone have questions?

2. Activity (20 minutes)

Script

We begin this new season with a close look at the reaction of the apostle Thomas to news that the crucified Jesus has risen from the dead and appeared to the other disciples. Let's turn to John 20:24–29 for the details. *(Have a teammate read the passage aloud while participants read along in their Bibles.)*

Thomas was not a person who easily accepted the word of others. He not only had to see the marks of the nails in Jesus's hands for himself but also insisted that he must touch Jesus's wounds. The apostle's disbelief was profound. Yet how many of us who learn of someone's death are left in shock and disbelief?

The way you and I respond to news surrounding the loss of someone is rooted in our family of origin's ideas and rules about death and how to respond to it. Today's exercise visits the past. Let's open the *Journal* to Marking the Route for session 1.

Exercise

Script

With a partner, you will complete these statements in your own words:

- My name is ______________________.
- The first family member whose death I recall was my _____________, who died when I was _____ years old.
- The rules about dealing with death that I remember from childhood are . . .
- The person who laid down the rules was . . .
- The rules taught me that God . . .

(On-site) Here's how sharing works:

1. Find a partner—preferably someone you don't know well. *(Continue when pairs are formed.)*
2. Decide who speaks first.
3. You each have about four minutes to tell your story with the statement stems.
4. Listening is an important part of being a participant, so please don't interrupt while your partner shares their story.
5. Change speakers when I signal. I will also signal when time is up.
6. Are there any questions before we begin? *(Pause to answer questions.)*
7. The first speaker's time begins now. *(Signal at 4 minutes and 8 minutes, which ends the exercise.)*
8. Now let's form a circle *(or other seating plan)* for faith-sharing questions. *(Continue when all are seated.)*

(Online) *Give the group time to ponder the exercise questions while you assign breakout rooms and time limit. Then give the following instructions.*

Here's how online sharing works:

1. You will be sent to a breakout room. Click the accept button to get there.
2. Introduce yourself to your partner and decide who speaks first.
3. You each have about four minutes to tell your story with the statement stems.
4. Listening is an important part of being a participant, so please don't interrupt while your partner shares their story.
5. A prompt will appear a minute before you automatically return to the main room for faith-sharing instructions.
6. I will now send you to your breakout rooms. *(Provide access. Continue when all group members have returned to the main room.)*

3. Faith Sharing (35 minutes)

Script

Before we begin the faith-sharing segment, let's review the Guide to Group Etiquette found in the *Journal*, page 52. *(Review the guide.)* Does anyone have questions?

(Online) *If needed, assign subgroups and time limit for faith-sharing breakout rooms. Then provide access. Participants will automatically return to the main room for the Summary.*

Questions on today's theme: Believing

As the scripture story shows, disbelief can accompany our losses.

1. When did your loved one's death become real for you? Explain.
2. In what way, if any, did the faith of your departed loved one influence your beliefs?
3. How did your belief in God affect your departed loved one? Give an example.

4. Summary (5 minutes)

- Comment on what the group or subgroups accomplished today.
- Show the *Journal's* Guidepost Bible citation and the Soul Work. Encourage everyone to commit to a time each week to connect to the Lord in this way.
- Announce the next session: Path to Understanding: *Knock and the Door Shall Be Opened.*
- Pray the Prayer to the Giver of Hope (group listens and prays silently):

O loving God,
spirit of consolation and giver of hope,
we thank you for the gift of your faithful people who join us today.
We ask you to bless and keep them in your care.
Let us also pray for the souls of our departed loved ones.
(Pause so that group members may call these to mind.)
May perpetual light shine upon them and bring eternal rest.
We ask this through Christ our Lord.
Amen. *(Make the Sign of the Cross.)*

- Wish everyone a blessed week.

5. Fellowship Break (On-site 30 minutes)

Schedule as desired: before the session begins, before faith sharing, or as a finale.

Season Three

Session 2

Path to Understanding

Theme: Knock and the Door Shall Be Opened

On-site items needed:

» sign-in materials (name tags, pencils, attendance sheet, and signs)
» pre-session music/player
» focal point
» Bibles
» tissue boxes
» color markers

1. Opening (20 minutes)

- Welcome the group to Session 2: Path to Understanding: *Knock and the Door Shall Be Opened.*
- **(On-site)** Thank those who brought refreshments.
- Begin the session with the Sign of the Cross.
    - **(On-site)** Pray the Seasons of Hope Prayer together.
    - **(Online)** A team member offers the Seasons of Hope Prayer aloud while the group joins in silently.
- Invite participants to state their name and that of the deceased, their relationship, and when the loss occurred. Give an example: "My name is (Jack), and I lost (Linda), my (wife), (six months) ago."
- Ask for God-wink stories from the week or insights from the Soul Work.
- Invite sharing of favorite faith or grief-related items.

2. Activity (20 minutes)

Script

The grief of losing a loved one can be emotionally and spiritually crippling if we do not seek Jesus. His healing power is present for those who mourn but is never forced on anyone. When we pray, we spiritually knock on the door to God's heavenly kingdom. Let's turn to **Matthew 7:7–11** to learn how to get a reply. *(Have a teammate read the passage aloud while participants read along in their Bibles.)*

Jesus tells us to ask our heavenly Father for what we seek. When we ask in Jesus's name, it is as if we send him to do the knocking for us.

Exercise

(On-site) Provide pencils and markers.

Script

Jesus wants to be invited into your sorrow, so he will knock at your door. Since you are here, it seems that you have already heard him knocking. When you open the door of your heart to him, you have taken the first step toward healing.

Let's open the *Journal* to Marking the Route for session 2.

1. In your mind's eye, conjure up an image of Jesus at your door. Write down a description of what you see or sketch him.
2. Ask Jesus for something you want that will ease your grief.

Take about ten minutes for this. I will signal when it's time to begin faith sharing.
(Online) *If needed, assign faith-sharing breakout rooms and time limit during writing exercise. Provide access after the signal. Participants will automatically return to the main room for the Summary.*

3. Faith Sharing (35 minutes)

Script

Jesus tells us to pray with confidence. Yet, when our hearts are broken, sometimes our prayer life can be put to the test.

Questions on today's theme: Knock and the Door Shall Be Opened

1. Since your loss, how hard have you been knocking on Jesus's door? Explain.

2. What type of consolation or blessing has God given you recently? Did you ask for it, or was it a surprise?
3. In what way has Jesus been knocking at your door? Give an example.

4. Summary (5 minutes)

- Comment on what the group or subgroups accomplished today.
- Announce the next session: Obstacles on the Journey: *Our Infirmities.*
- Encourage everyone to do the session's Soul Work in the *Journal* this week.
- Pray the Prayer to the Giver of Hope (group listens and prays silently):

  O loving God,
  spirit of consolation and giver of hope,
  we thank you for the gift of your faithful people who join us today.
  We ask you to bless and keep them in your care.
  Let us also pray for the souls of our departed lived ones.
  (Pause so that group members may call these to mind.)
  May perpetual light shine upon them and bring eternal rest.
  We ask this through Christ our Lord.
  Amen. *(Make the Sign of the Cross.)*

- Wish everyone a blessed week.

5. Fellowship Break (On-site 30 minutes)

Schedule as desired: before the session begins, before faith sharing, or as a finale.

Season Three

Session 3

Obstacles on the Journey

Theme: Our Infirmities

On-site items needed:

» sign-in materials
» pre-session music/player
» focal point
» Bibles
» pencils
» tissue boxes

On-site and online item:

» "You Raise Me Up" by Josh Groban on *Closer* (CD) (optional)

1. Opening (20 minutes)

- Welcome the group to Session 3: Obstacles on the Journey: *Our Infirmities.*
- **(On-site)** Thank those who brought refreshments.
- Begin the session with the Sign of the Cross.
    - **(On-site)** Pray the Seasons of Hope Prayer together.
    - **(Online)** A team member offers the Seasons of Hope Prayer aloud while the group joins in silently.
- **(On-site)** Explain the purpose of the Network Directory in the *Journal.*
- Ask for God-wink stories from the week or insights from the Soul Work.
- Invite sharing of favorite faith or grief-related items.

2. Activity (20 minutes)

Script

What if Jesus stood before you and lifted the heavy burden of sorrow from you? What would you do? Let's turn to **Luke 13:10–13** for a similar story from his day. *(Have a teammate read the passage aloud while participants read along in their Bibles.)*

Like the woman who was unable to stand erect, we get weighed down by carrying the heavy burden of grief. Others saw the burden of her infirmity, but only the Lord knew how to lighten her load. The exercise we are about to do brings Jesus's tender touch to the wounds of our grief.

(Proceed with the music meditation and exercise or do only the exercise)

Script (music meditation)

Begin playing "You Raise Me Up." (Online) *Use Share Screen.*
Sit back and relax as you listen to Josh Groban sing "You Raise Me Up." Imagine he is singing to Jesus. Let the song become your prayer of gratitude to God.

Exercise

(On-site) Provide pencils.

SEASON Three

Script

Let's open the *Journal* to Marking the Route for session 3.

1. Think about how it will feel when the Lord heals your wounded spirit.
2. Jot down your thoughts.

I will signal when it's time to begin faith sharing.

(Online) *If needed, assign faith-sharing breakout rooms and time limit during writing exercise. Provide access after the signal. Participants will automatically return to the main room for the Summary.*

3. Faith Sharing (40 minutes)

Script

Grieving is a normal reaction to losing a loved one. But the unpredictable emotions that come with a broken heart don't feel normal. They can wound our spirit and weigh us down.

Questions on today's theme: Our Infirmities

1. What has weighed you down the most since your loved one died? Explain.
2. How has the Lord raised you up from that weighed-down feeling? If he hasn't yet, what would you like him to do for you?
3. What do you do to ease or avoid the triggers that create bouts of tears or that weighed-down feeling?

4. Summary (5 minutes)

- Comment on what the group or subgroups accomplished today.
- Announce the next session: Path to Inner Healing: *Blinders to Faith.*
- Encourage everyone to do the session's Soul Work this week.
- Pray the Prayer to the Giver of Hope (group listens and prays silently):

  O loving God,
  spirit of consolation and giver of hope,
  we thank you for the gift of your faithful people who join us today.
  We ask you to bless and keep them in your care.
  Let us also pray for the souls of our departed loved ones.
  (Pause so that group members may call these to mind.)
  May perpetual light shine upon them and bring eternal rest.
  We ask this through Christ our Lord.
  Amen. *(Make the Sign of the Cross.)*

- Wish everyone a blessed week.

5. Fellowship Break (On-site 30 minutes)

Schedule as desired: before the session begins, before faith sharing, or as a finale.

Season Three

Session 4

Path to Inner Healing

Theme: Blinders to Faith

On-site items needed:

» sign-in materials
» pre-session music/player
» focal point
» Bibles
» tissue boxes
» pencils

1. Opening (20 minutes)

- Welcome the group to Session 4: Path to Inner Healing: *Blinders to Faith.*
- **(On-site)** Thank those who brought refreshments.
- Begin the session with the Sign of the Cross.
    - **(On-site)** Pray the Seasons of Hope Prayer together.
    - **(Online)** A team member offers the Seasons of Hope Prayer aloud while the group joins in silently.
- Ask for God-wink stories from the week or insights from the Soul Work.
- Invite sharing of favorite faith or grief-related items.

2. Activity (15 minutes)

Script

Some who mourn don't even consider calling upon Jesus to ease their suffering. Scripture, however, highlights unique individuals who publicly seek the Lord's endless mercy and compassion. Let's turn to **Luke 18:35–43** for one man's story. *(Have a teammate read the passage aloud while participants read along in their Bibles.)*

The beggar who seeks sight is much like the grief-stricken who yearn for insight into their own predicament. Each situation demands trust in God.

Exercise

(On-site) Provide pencils.

Script

Let's open the *Journal* to Marking the Route for session 4.

1. Take time to think about the blind man's encounter with Jesus. What strikes you most about the story?
2. Take the next few minutes to write a letter to God about how you are like or unlike the blind man as you call upon Jesus to ease your suffering. Ask for something that will help you get through the grieving process.

I will signal when it's time to begin faith sharing.

(Online) *If needed, assign faith-sharing breakout rooms and time limit during writing exercise. Provide access after the signal. Participants will automatically return to the main room for the Summary.*

3. Faith Sharing (45 minutes)

Script

Others rebuked the blind man when he sought the Lord's help, yet he persisted and was healed because of his faith.

Questions on today's theme: Blinders to Faith

1. Is your faith in the Lord the same or different since losing your loved one? Explain.
2. What way, if any, has a sacrament or sacred tradition helped you see God's mercy and compassion more clearly now? Give an example.

3. What spiritual lessons about perseverance have you learned on your grief journey? Explain.

4. Summary (5 minutes)

- Comment on what the group or subgroups accomplished today.
- Announce the next session: Way of Suffering: *His Wound of Love*.
- Encourage everyone to do the session's Soul Work in the *Journal* this week.
- Pray the Prayer to the Giver of Hope (group listens and prays silently):

    O loving God,
    spirit of consolation and giver of hope,
    we thank you for the gift of your faithful people who join us today.
    We ask you to bless and keep them in your care.
    Let us also pray for the souls of our departed loved ones.
    (Pause so that group members may call these to mind.)
    May perpetual light shine upon them and bring eternal rest.
    We ask this through Christ our Lord.
    Amen. *(Make the Sign of the Cross.)*

- Wish everyone a blessed week.

5. Fellowship Break (On-site 30 minutes)

Schedule as desired: before the session begins, before faith sharing, or as a finale.

Season Three

Session 5

Way of Suffering

Theme: His Wound of Love

On-site items needed:

» sign-in materials
» presession music/player
» Bibles
» tissue boxes
» pencils

On-site and online items needed:

» focal point (Sacred Heart of Jesus image—a framed image, prayer card, or digital picture from the internet)
» *Maundy Thursday: Gregorian Chant* (CD) by the Monastic Choir of St. Peter's Abbey or *Requiem* (CD) by the Priestly Fraternity of St. Peter (optional)

1. Opening (15 minutes)

- Welcome the group to Session 5: Way of Suffering: *His Wound of Love*.
- **(On-site)** Thank those who brought refreshments.
- Begin the session with the Sign of the Cross.
    - **(On-site)** Pray the Seasons of Hope Prayer together.
    - **(Online)** A team member offers the Seasons of Hope Prayer aloud while the group joins in silently.
- Ask for God-wink stories from the week or insights from the Soul Work.
- Invite sharing of favorite faith or grief-related items.

2. Activity (15 minutes)

Script

The suffering and heartache of losing a precious loved one can make us feel incredibly wounded, so much so that we may wonder if we'll ever be healed or feel whole again. It's in those dark moments that we must allow our faith in Jesus, who poured out his love for us on the Cross, to guide us.

Let's turn to **1 Peter 2:20b–24** to look at the condition of suffering as an inevitable path for those who follow in the footsteps of our Lord and Savior, the guardian of our wounded hearts. *(Have a teammate read the passage aloud while participants read along in their Bibles.)*

St. Peter's letter reminds us that Jesus is Love Incarnate and that by his wounds there was and always will be healing for those who believe. Jesus called his apostles and us into a more perfect union with his loving heart. A popular devotion inspired by St. Margaret Mary's visions of Jesus in the seventeenth century can help us do that. Jesus asked, among other things, to be honored in the symbol of his heart of flesh. We know the image as his Sacred Heart. Today's exercise will help you ponder the sacred wound of Jesus's heart and the promise of love, grace, and healing that flow from it.

(Proceed with the music and writing exercise or do only the exercise.)

Script (optional music)

Begin playing Maundy Thursday *or* Requiem. **(Online)** *Use Share Screen.*
To set the mood, sacred music from the Church of the Middle Ages, Gregorian chant, will accompany the exercise. Its rhythmic, monotone singing of the liturgy alternates between soloist and monastic choir.

Exercise

(On-site) Provide pencils. (Online) Display Sacred Heart image via Share Screen.

Script

Open the *Journal* to Marking the Route for session 5.

1. Gaze at the image of the Sacred Heart. Observe the wound inflicted as Jesus hung lifelessly on the Cross.
2. Imagine the burst of blood and water that flowed out as symbols of his love—the precious Blood of the Eucharist and the holy waters of Baptism.
3. Think about Jesus's desire to share his heartfelt love, grace, and healing with you now.
4. Write to him about what comes to mind.

I will signal when it's time to begin faith sharing.

(Online) *If needed, assign faith-sharing breakout rooms and time limit during the writing exercise. Provide access after the signal. Participants will automatically return to the main room for the Summary.*

3. Faith Sharing (45 minutes)

Questions on today's theme: His Wound of Love

1. Jesus's Sacred Heart burns with love for you. In what positive or negative way has the loss of your loved one affected your awareness of Jesus's love? Explain.
2. What wound of your broken heart have you brought, or would you like to bring, to Jesus's Sacred Heart? Does it need love, grace, healing? Give details.
3. The Sacred Heart devotion invites us to keep a holy hour, partake in frequent Communion, and otherwise adore the heart of Jesus. What acts of faith lift your spirit?

4. Summary (5 minutes)

SEASON Three

- Comment on what the group or subgroups accomplished today.
- Announce the last session of this season: Final Destination: *Do Not Weep*.
- Ask participants to bring an item next week that reminds them of the faith of their loved one.
- Encourage everyone to do the session's Soul Work this week.
- Pray the Prayer to the Giver of Hope (group listens and prays silently):

  O loving God,
  spirit of consolation and giver of hope,
  we thank you for the gift of your faithful people who join us today.
  We ask you to bless and keep them in your care.
  Let us also pray for the souls of our departed loved ones.
  (Pause so that group members may call these to mind.)
  May perpetual light shine upon them and bring eternal rest.
  We ask this through Christ our Lord.
  Amen. *(Make the Sign of the Cross.)*

- Wish everyone a blessed week.

5. Fellowship Break (On-site 30 minutes)

Schedule as desired: before the session begins, before faith sharing, or as a finale.

Season Three

Session 6

Final Destination

Theme: Do Not Weep

On-site items needed:

» sign-in materials
» pre-session music/player
» focal point table for items brought by group
» chairs formed in a circle that includes the table
» Bibles
» tissue boxes
» pencils
» a reminder of the faith of your loved one

On-site and online items:

» camera (optional)
» Season Survey

1. Opening (10 minutes)

- Welcome the group to Session 6: Final Destination: *Do Not Weep*.
- **(On-site)** Thank those who brought refreshments.
- Begin the session with the Sign of the Cross.
    - **(On-site)** Pray the Seasons of Hope Prayer together.
    - **(Online)** A team member offers the Seasons of Hope Prayer aloud while the group joins in silently.
- **(On-site)** Ask all to join in a group photo (optional).
- **(Online)** Ask all to smile for a group photo on screen (optional).
- Use the script below for sharing of items related to loved ones.

2. Activity (30 minutes)

Exercise

Script

Each week in session we have honored our deceased loved ones with word and prayer. Today we go a step further. You will each have a chance to

1. Show us something that reminds you of the faith of your departed loved one and tell why it's special to you.
2. **(On-site)** Then bring the item to the table with the image of Jesus. This brief walk is a symbol of your journey with us these past weeks.

Who would like to go first? *(Continue after everyone has shared their special item.)*

Thank you for sharing. It's nice to know more about your loved ones. Now we'll focus on scripture.

SEASON Three

Scripture

Script

The love Jesus brings to our lives through our loved ones may not be memorialized in great works like the Bible, but we take comfort in listening to its accounts of his divine kindness to those who mourn. Let's turn to **Luke 7:11–17** for such a story. *(Have a teammate read the passage aloud while participants read along in their Bibles.)*

Jesus didn't wait for the grieving widow to seek his help; instead, he reached out to her in love. Those of us who desire his compassion surely won't be disappointed.

(Online) *If needed, assign subgroups and time limit for faith-sharing breakout rooms. Then provide access. Participants will automatically return to the main room for the Summary.*

3. Faith Sharing (40 minutes)

Questions on today's theme: Do Not Weep

1. In what way, if any, has Jesus tended to your tears of sorrow? If your grief isn't filled with sorrow, how has he helped you?
2. How have you let Jesus know that you appreciate his compassion? Explain.
3. How has sharing your faith with others at Seasons of Hope made a difference on your grief journey? Explain.

4. Summary (15 minutes)

- Comment on group accomplishments this season.
- Share future Seasons of Hope offerings and ask participants to spread the word.
- Encourage everyone to do the Soul Work in the *Journal* this week.
- **(On-site)** Have participants complete and submit the *Journal's* Season Survey.
- **(Online)** Have participants complete and return the Season Survey emailed to them for this purpose.
- Pray the Prayer to the Giver of Hope *(ask everyone to pray silently but to say the name of their beloved aloud during the pause):*

  O loving God,
  spirit of consolation and giver of hope,
  we thank you for the gift of your faithful people who join us today.
  We ask you to bless and keep them in your care.
  Let us also pray for the souls of our departed loved ones.
  (Name your beloved and pause while others name theirs.)
  May perpetual light shine upon them and bring eternal rest.
  We ask this through Christ our Lord.
  Amen. *(Make the Sign of the Cross.)*

- Wish everyone well.

5. Fellowship Break (On-site 30 minutes)

Schedule as desired: before the session begins, before faith sharing, or as a finale.

Season Four

Session 1

Point of Departure

Theme: Last Encounter

On-site items needed:

» sign-in materials (name tags, markers, attendance sheet, and signs)
» Season Four *Journals* for group
» pre-session music/player
» focal point (image of Jesus)
» Bibles
» tissue boxes
» timer or watch
» bell (optional)
» refreshment sign-up sheet (optional)

1. Opening (20 minutes)

- On behalf of the team, welcome the group to Session 1: Point of Departure: *Last Encounter*.
- Begin the session with the Sign of the Cross.
  - **(On-site)** Pray together the Seasons of Hope Prayer on the back cover of the *Journal*.
  - **(Online)** A team member offers the Seasons of Hope Prayer aloud while the group joins in silently.
- Keep introductions brief. Invite participants to say their name and relation to their deceased loved one. Give an example: "My name is (Helen), and I lost my (sister)." Assure

them that they will share more during the session.

- Use the script below to explain the Seasons of Hope program, *Journals*, and any housekeeping details.

Script

"Blessed are those who mourn," our Lord assured us, "for they will be comforted" (Mt 5:4). Seasons of Hope brings us together to share in God's love. The support of this community will enable you to give voice to your unique journey and take a step toward healing and spiritual growth.

You are an expert on your grief. We aren't here to teach you about its stages. You meet them on your journey. Instead, we will explore mourning through scripture, prayer, reflection, and faith sharing. We will help you focus on your relationship with the Lord and the many ways his Church offers consolation. Along the way, you will find Jesus in others who mourn and within your own heart.

We use the Bible each week. The *Journal's* Guidepost page has the Bible citation of the passage you read here and again at home. **(On-site)** Does anyone need to borrow a Bible now? *(Have a teammate provide them.)*

Please have your *Journal* handy too. We use it for our opening exercise in group and for Soul Work at home after each session. The Soul Work gives a fresh perspective on the scripture reading. Plus, it allows you to reflect on your relationship with the Lord, write about your loss, and share in a consoling tradition of the Church.

The group session officially concludes with the Summary, which sends you forth with the Prayer to the Giver of Hope.

Now for some housekeeping details:

- We start promptly each week, so please arrive a few minutes early.
- If you can't make a session, please tell us .
- Please silence your cell phone.
- **(Online)** Please mute your speaker if your room gets noisy.
- **(On-site)** Restrooms are located in the . . .
- Each session, you are invited to show one of your favorite faith or grief-related items. It could be a book, poem, prayer, song, website, devotional item, etc.
- **(On-site)** The fellowship break is at *(indicate time)*. It's our informal time to share refreshments and get to know each other as neighbors and community members.
- (**On-site** optional) We need help with refreshments. Please sign up to bring one plate of snacks sometime this season. Thank you. This week *(give names)* brought snacks. Let's offer our thanks with a round of applause.

Does anyone have questions?

2. Activity (20 minutes)

Script

When our departed loved ones are still with us, it is impossible to imagine life without them. Questions about eternal life also arise. At the last Passover meal, the disciples faced the same concerns when Jesus spoke about leaving them behind. Let's turn to **John 14:1–8** to hear what transpired. *(Have a teammate read the passage aloud while participants read along in their Bibles.)*

The dismay Thomas shared with the Lord opens the door for Philip, another disciple, to express his concerns about losing Jesus. Questions about eternal life occupy all of us—sometimes quite intensely, as when a loved one dies. Our views about what happens to the soul when someone dies start forming when we are children. The next exercise focuses on what your parents and other family members taught you about life after death and their way of grieving.

Exercise

Script

Let's open the *Journal* to Marking the Route for session 1. With a partner, you will complete these statements in your own words:

- My name is ________________________ .
- Things my parents/family believed about life after death include . . .
- When someone we loved died, my parents/family taught me that God . . .
- To ease their own grief, my parents/family would . . .
- Back then, when I was sad over losing someone dear, I would . . .

(On-site) Here's how sharing works:

1. Find a partner—preferably someone you don't know well. *(Continue when pairs are formed.)*
2. Decide who speaks first.
3. You each have about four minutes to tell your story with the statement stems.
4. Listening is an important part of being a participant, so please don't interrupt while your partner shares their story.
5. Change speakers when I signal. I will also signal when time is up.
6. Are there any questions before we begin? *(Pause to answer questions.)*
7. The first speaker's time begins now. *(Signal at 4 minutes and 8 minutes, which ends the exercise.)*
8. Now let's form a circle *(or other seating plan)* for faith-sharing questions. *(Continue when all are seated.)*

(Online) *Give the group time to ponder the exercise questions while you assign breakout rooms and time limit. Then give the following instructions.*

Here's how online sharing works:

1. You will be sent to a breakout room. Click the accept button to get there.
2. Introduce yourself to your partner and decide who speaks first.
3. You each have about four minutes to tell your story with the statement stems.
4. Listening is an important part of being a participant, so please don't interrupt while your partner shares their story.
5. A prompt will appear a minute before you automatically return to the main room for faith-sharing instructions.
6. I will now send you to your breakout rooms. *(Provide access. Continue when all group members have returned to the main room.)*

3. Faith Sharing (35 minutes)

Script

Before we begin the faith-sharing segment, let's review the Guide to Group Etiquette found in the *Journal*, page 52. *(Review the guide.)* Does anyone have questions?

(Online) *If needed, assign subgroups and time limit for faith-sharing breakout rooms. Then provide access. Participants will automatically return to the main room for the Summary.*

Questions on today's theme: Last Encounter

At the Last Supper, Jesus wanted the disciples to have faith in him and not worry about the future. He spoke of reunion with them in the Father's house.

1. Has worry played a major or minor role in mourning your loved one? Explain.
2. In what way has belief in God helped you cope with being left behind?
3. Has your loss made you think about the eternal dwelling place God has for your loved one or you? If so, what have you concluded?

4. Summary (5 minutes)

- Comment on what the group or subgroups accomplished today.
- Show the *Journal's* Guidepost Bible citation and Soul Work. Encourage everyone to commit to a time each week to connect to the Lord in this way.
- Announce the next session: Path to Understanding: *The Garden of Gethsemane.*
- Pray the Prayer to the Giver of Hope (group listens and prays silently):

O loving God,
spirit of consolation and giver of hope,
we thank you for the gift of your faithful people who join us today.
We ask you to bless and keep them in your care.
Let us also pray for the souls of our departed loved ones.
(Pause so that group members may call these to mind.)
May perpetual light shine upon them and bring eternal rest.
We ask this through Christ our Lord.
Amen. *(Make the Sign of the Cross.)*

- Wish everyone a blessed week.

5. Fellowship Break (On-site 30 minutes)

Schedule as desired: before the session begins, before faith sharing, or as a finale.

Season Four

Session 2

Path to Understanding

Theme: The Garden of Gethsemane

On-site items needed:

» sign-in materials (name tags, markers, attendance sheet, and signs)
» pre-session music/player
» focal point
» Bibles
» tissue boxes

On-site and online item:

» *Requiem* (CD) by the Priestly Fraternity of St. Peter (optional)

1. Opening (20 minutes)

» Welcome the group to Session 2: Path to Understanding: *The Garden of Gethsemane.*
» **(On-site)** Thank those who brought refreshments.
» Begin the session with the Sign of the Cross.
  * **(On-site)** Pray the Seasons of Hope Prayer together.
  * **(Online)** A team member offers the Seasons of Hope Prayer aloud while the group joins in silently.
» Invite participants to state their name and that of the deceased, their relationship, and when the loss occurred. Give an example: "My name is (Helen), and I lost (Kate), my (sister), (last November)."
» Ask for God-wink stories from the week or insights from the Soul Work.
» Invite sharing of favorite faith or grief-related items.

2. Activity (15 minutes)

Script

Mourning can trouble us deeply, bringing great sorrow to our hearts. When we feel betrayed and alone in our grief, we are not far from the agony Jesus suffered in the garden of Gethsemane. Let's turn to **Mark 14:32–42** to listen carefully to our Lord's ordeal. *(Have a teammate read the passage aloud while participants read along in their Bibles.)*

The remarkable scene in the garden reveals Jesus's way of coping. He prayed fervently to the Father as he struggled with what was to come, yet he desired above all else to fulfill the Father's will. The cup of suffering passes to his disciples today and tests even the most devout among us.

(Proceed with Requiem *and the writing exercise or do only the exercise.)*

Exercise

(On-site) Provide pencils.

Script

Let's open the *Journal* to Marking the Route for session 2.

1. Imagine being in a garden where you feel close to God.
2. Consider the things that the Father could help you with in your time of distress.
3. Make a list of those requests in the *Journal.*

I'll signal when it's time to begin faith sharing.

(Online) *If needed, assign faith-sharing breakout rooms and time limit during exercise. Provide access after the signal. Participants will automatically return to the main room for the Summary.*

3. Faith Sharing (40 minutes)

Questions on today's theme: The Garden of Gethsemane

1. If God were to answer one prayer that would ease your grief right now, what would it be? Explain.
2. Has your approach to prayer stayed the same or changed since your loss? Tell us about what practice of faith brings you the most comfort now.
3. Do you have friends like Peter, James, and John for support? Whether you do or not, what would you like someone to do to ease your grief?

4. Summary (5 minutes)

- Comment on what the group or subgroups accomplished today.
- Announce the next session: Obstacles on the Journey: *Crown of Thorns.*
- Encourage everyone to do the session's Soul Work in the *Journal* this week.
- Pray the Prayer to the Giver of Hope (group listens and prays silently):

  O loving God,
  spirit of consolation and giver of hope,
  we thank you for the gift of your faithful people who join us today.
  We ask you to bless and keep them in your care.
  Let us also pray for the souls of our departed loved ones.
  (Pause so that group members may call these to mind.)
  May perpetual light shine upon them and bring eternal rest.
  We ask this through Christ our Lord.
  Amen. *(Make the Sign of the Cross.)*

- Wish everyone a blessed week.

5. Fellowship Break (On-site 30 minutes)

Schedule as desired: before the session begins, before faith sharing, or as a finale.

Season Four

Session 3

Obstacles on the Journey

Theme: Crown of Thorns

On-site items needed:

» sign-in materials
» pre-session music/player
» focal point
» Bibles
» tissue boxes
» a rose with thorns (or a crown of thorns, perhaps from a passion play)
» pencils

Online item needed:

» an image of a rose with thorns or a crown of thorns

1. Opening (20 minutes)

- Welcome the group to Session 3: Obstacles on the Journey: *Crown of Thorns.*
- **(On-site)** Thank those who brought refreshments.
- Begin the session with the Sign of the Cross.
  - ⁕ **(On-site)** Pray the Seasons of Hope Prayer together.
  - ⁕ **(Online)** A team member offers the Seasons of Hope Prayer aloud while the group joins in silently.
- **(On-site)** Explain the purpose of the Network Directory in the *Journal.*
- Ask for God-wink stories from the week or insights from the Soul Work.
- Invite sharing of favorite faith or grief-related items.

2. Activity (15 minutes)

Script

It is hard to fathom the cruelty and physical pain Jesus experienced at the hands of his enemies. Some movies picture it for us, but a symbol of the Passion such as the crown of thorns can also help us imagine the Lord's suffering of mind, body, and soul. Let's turn to **John 19:1–3.** *(Have a teammate read the passage aloud while participants read along in their Bibles.)*

Grieving may not brutalize the body, but it does impact both our physical and mental health. Grieving also affects the health of our soul. Spiritually speaking, our suffering unites us more closely to Jesus. From that closeness comes the knowledge of who Jesus truly is.

Exercise

(On-site) Provide pencils.
(Online) Display rose or crown image via Share.

Script

The thorns used in the crown to torture Jesus were probably from a thorn plant not common to our experience. But most of us can relate to prickly thorns found on a rose bush. The rose is another popular symbol in Christianity. Because it is a perfect flower, it is an image of wisdom and a symbol of Christ.

With that in mind, let's open the *Journal* to Marking the Route for session 3.

1. Contemplate the crown of thorns *(or thorny rose)* that's on display. Reflect on Jesus's suffering and yours.
2. Then write to Jesus about how you deal with the emotional and spiritual pain of your grief.

I will signal when it's time to begin faith sharing.

(Online) *If needed, assign faith-sharing breakout rooms and time limit during writing exercise. Provide access after the signal. Participants will automatically return to the main room for the Summary.*

3. Faith Sharing (45 minutes)

Questions on today's theme: Crown of Thorns

1. When you think of your grief, what is the most painful part—the biggest thorn? Explain its effect on you.
2. When have you found, or wish you could find, Jesus (the rose) among the thorns? Explain.

3. Have you felt any easing of your pain recently? If so, explain what's different and what helps. If not, what could a friend do to help?

4. Summary (5 minutes)

- Comment on what the group or subgroups accomplished today.
- Announce the next session: Path to Inner Healing: *Gift of Caring.*
- Encourage everyone to do the session's Soul Work in the *Journal* this week.
- Pray the Prayer to the Giver of Hope (group listens and prays silently):

> O loving God,
> spirit of consolation and giver of hope,
> we thank you for the gift of your faithful people who join us today.
> We ask you to bless and keep them in your care.
> Let us also pray for the souls of our departed loved ones.
> *(Pause so that group members may call these to mind.)*
> May perpetual light shine upon them and bring eternal rest.
> We ask this through Christ our Lord.
> Amen. *(Make the Sign of the Cross.)*

- Wish everyone a blessed week.

5. Fellowship Break (On-site 30 minutes)

Schedule as desired: before the session begins, before faith sharing, or as a finale.

Season Four

Session 4

Path to Inner Healing

Theme: Gift of Caring

On-site items needed:

» sign-in materials
» pre-session music/player
» focal point
» Bibles
» pencils
» tissue boxes

1. Opening (15 minutes)

- Welcome the group to Session 4: Path to Inner Healing: *Gift of Caring.*
- **(On-site)** Thank those who brought refreshments.
- Begin the session with the Sign of the Cross.
    - **(On-site)** Pray the Seasons of Hope Prayer together.
    - **(Online)** A team member offers the Seasons of Hope Prayer aloud while the group joins in silently.
- Ask for God-wink stories from the week or insights from the Soul Work.
- Invite sharing of favorite faith or grief-related items.

2. Activity (20 minutes)

Script

You know who your friends are when misfortune befalls you. At the end of Jesus's journey, only the youngest apostle, John, joined Mary and the faithful women disciples who stood at the foot of the Cross. Let's turn to **John 19:25–30** for the details. *(Have a teammate read the passage aloud while participants read along in their Bibles.)*

In that era, a poor widow would have had a hard life if she did not have a child to support her. No wonder Jesus wanted his mother to have his disciple John as a son. Jesus cared about Mary's welfare, but he also had a message for his followers: the Blessed Virgin Mary was to be mother to all God's children, and, like John, we are to care for others in his name.

Exercise

Script

Let's open the *Journal* to Marking the Route for session 4.

1. Write a letter to Jesus. Let him know who has stood by you in your time of sorrow. Express your gratitude for the gift of their concern and their acts of kindness.
2. If no one comes to mind, write about the gift of Seasons of Hope.

I will signal when it's time to begin faith sharing.

(Online) *If needed, assign faith-sharing breakout rooms and time limit during writing exercise. Provide access after the signal. Participants will automatically return to the main room for the Summary.*

3. Faith Sharing (40 minutes)

Script

Jesus had unfinished business on his mind during the last moments of his life. When he called upon John to console his dear mother, the message was clear. His followers tend to the brokenhearted.

Questions on today's theme: Gift of Caring

1. Can you give an example of an act of kindness that someone did for you during the wake or funeral for your loved one? Explain how it made you feel.

2. Do you have an example of a kind act that is more recent? Tell us about it. If one doesn't come to mind, what would you like someone to do for you?
3. How would you reach out to someone you care about who is newly bereaved? Would you act any differently than before your loss? Explain.

4. Summary (5 minutes)

- Comment on what the group or subgroups accomplished today.
- Announce the next session: Way of Suffering: *Why Have You Forsaken Me?*
- Encourage everyone to do the session's Soul Work in the *Journal* this week.
- Pray the Prayer to the Giver of Hope (group listens and prays silently):

  O loving God,
  spirit of consolation and giver of hope,
  we thank you for the gift of your faithful people who join us today.
  We ask you to bless and keep them in your care.
  Let us also pray for the souls of our departed loved ones.
  (Pause so that group members may call these to mind.)
  May perpetual light shine upon them and bring eternal rest.
  We ask this through Christ our Lord.
  Amen. *(Make the Sign of the Cross.)*

- Wish everyone a blessed week.

5. Fellowship Break (On-site 30 minutes)

Schedule as desired: before the session begins, before faith sharing, or as a finale.

Season Four

Session 5

Way of Suffering

Theme: Why Have You Forsaken Me?

On-site items needed:

» sign-in materials
» pre-session music/player
» Bibles
» tissue boxes
» pencils

On-site and online item needed:

» focal point (Divine Mercy image—framed picture, prayer card, or downloaded image)

1. Opening (15 minutes)

- Welcome the group to Session 5: Way of Suffering: *Why Have You Forsaken Me?*
- **(On-site)** Thank those who brought refreshments.
- Begin the session with the Sign of the Cross.
    - **(On-site)** Pray the Seasons of Hope Prayer together.
    - **(Online)** A team member offers the Seasons of Hope Prayer aloud while the group joins in silently.
- Ask for God-wink stories from the week or insights from the Soul Work.
- Invite sharing of favorite faith or grief-related items.

2. Activity (20 minutes)

Script

The death of a loved one can blindside us, whether it is sudden or comes after prolonged suffering. We can feel forsaken by the unfairness of life, medical personnel, the deceased, onlookers, and even God. In a sense, something within us has died. It's called trust. And for many of us who feel abandoned, trust in our own self also gets shaky. We can't imagine life without our beloved.

This week we enter the Way of Suffering segment of Seasons of Hope. We look to our suffering Savior's last moments on the Cross and his words to the Father that address feeling forsaken.

Let's turn to **Mark 15:22–34** to set the scene. *(Have a teammate read the passage aloud while participants read along in their Bibles.)*

It is believed that Jesus's last words, "My God, my God, why have you forsaken me?" are rooted in Psalm 22, which acknowledges the despair of death but also gives hope for deliverance. It foretells the suffering of the Messiah. Even in agony, Jesus had trust in the mercy of God the Father, for his mission was always to do his Father's will. By dying on the Cross, our merciful Savior removed the barriers between us and God.

The Divine Mercy devotion of today, inspired by St. Faustina's visions of Jesus almost a century ago, reminds us that when we call upon Jesus with trust, we receive his mercy. What a gift God's mercy is in the midst of our grieving!

Exercise

(On-site) Provide pencils.
(Online) Display Divine Mercy image via Share Screen.

SEASON **Four**

Script

Let's open the *Journal* to Marking the Route for session 5. We'll look at one part of the Divine Mercy devotion, its image.

1. Notice Jesus's expression, posture, gestures, the symbols of holiness, and the rays of his merciful fountain of grace. What catches your eye?
2. Think about the message, "Jesus, I trust in You."
3. Let Jesus speak to your heart.
4. Then share your thoughts in writing with him.

I will signal when it's time to begin faith sharing.

(Online) *If needed, assign faith-sharing breakout rooms and time limit during writing exercise. Provide access after the signal. Participants will automatically return to the main room for the Summary.*

3. Faith Sharing (45 minutes)

Questions on today's theme: Why Have You Forsaken Me?

1. Has your grief ever made you feel forsaken by the unfairness of life, people, or even God? If so, how has your faith helped you cope?
2. The Divine Mercy devotion tells us to ask Jesus for mercy, be merciful, and completely trust in him. Which part is easy for you since your loss? Which part is difficult? Explain.
3. What act of faith or devotion, if any, helps when you're feeling lonely or abandoned? Explain.

4. Summary (5 minutes)

- Comment on what the group or subgroups accomplished today.
- Announce the season's last session: Final Destination: *Be My Witnesses.*
- Ask participants to bring an item next week that symbolizes their love for their departed one.
- Encourage everyone to do the session's Soul Work in the *Journal* this week.
- Pray the Prayer to the Giver of Hope (group listens and prays silently):

    O loving God,
    spirit of consolation and giver of hope,
    we thank you for the gift of your faithful people who join us today.
    We ask you to bless and keep them in your care.
    Let us also pray for the souls of our departed loved ones.
    (Pause so that group members may call these to mind.)
    May perpetual light shine upon them and bring eternal rest.
    We ask this through Christ our Lord.
    Amen. *(Make the Sign of the Cross.)*

- Wish everyone a blessed week.

5. Fellowship Break (On-site 30 minutes)

Schedule as desired: before the session begins, before faith sharing, or as a finale.

Season Four

Session 6

Final Destination

Theme: Be My Witnesses

On-site items needed:

» sign-in materials
» pre-session music/player
» focal point table for items brought by group
» chairs formed in a circle that includes the table
» Bibles
» tissue boxes
» a reminder of the love shared with the departed
» pencils

On-site and online items:

» Season Survey
» camera (optional)

1. Opening (10 minutes)

- Welcome the group to Session 6: Final Destination: *Be My Witnesses*.
- **(On-site)** Thank those who brought refreshments.
- Begin the session with the Sign of the Cross.
    - ⁎ **(On-site)** Pray the Seasons of Hope Prayer together.
    - ⁎ **(Online)** A team member offers the Seasons of Hope Prayer aloud while the group joins in silently.
- **(On-site)** Ask all to join in a group photo (optional).
- **(Online)** Ask all to smile for a group photo on screen (optional).
- Use the script below for sharing of items related to loved ones.

2. Activity (35 minutes)

Exercise

Script

Each week in session we have honored our deceased loved ones with word and prayer. Today we go a step further. You will each have a chance to

1. Show us something that reminds you of the love you shared with your departed loved one and tell why it's special to you.
2. **(On-site)** Then bring the item to the table with the image of Jesus. This brief walk is a symbol of your journey with us these past weeks.

Who would like to go first? *(Continue after everyone has shared their special item.)*

Thank you for sharing. It's nice to know more about your loved ones. Now we'll focus on scripture.

Scripture

Script

Your stories are wonderful examples of the power of love. And love was the center of the Lord's teaching. Jesus shared a final teaching as he was about to ascend to heaven. Let's turn to **Acts 1:6–11** to learn what he said. *(Have a teammate read the passage aloud while participants read along in their Bibles.)*

The grieving apostles, like many of us, had questions about the future. Jesus's reply affirmed what mourning teaches us: what lies ahead is a mystery to us. Nevertheless, we are to be his witnesses.

SEASON Four

(Online) *If needed, assign subgroups and time limit for faith-sharing breakout rooms. Then provide access. Participants will automatically return to the main room for the Summary.*

3. Faith Sharing (40 minutes)

Script

By participating in Seasons of Hope, you have been the Lord's witnesses.

Questions on today's theme: Be My Witnesses

1. Has being with others who mourn given you hope? In what way?
2. What hope have you shared with them?
3. How might you take what you have learned about grief and the power of faith and use it as a witness in our community of believers or beyond?

4. Summary (15 minutes)

- Comment on group accomplishments this season.
- Share future Seasons of Hope offerings and ask participants to spread the word.
- Encourage everyone to do the session's Soul Work in the Journal this week.
- **(On-site)** Have participants complete and submit the *Journal's* Season Survey.
- **(Online)** Have participants complete and return the Season Survey emailed to them for this purpose.
- Pray the Prayer to the Giver of Hope *(ask everyone to pray silently but to say the name of their beloved aloud during the pause)*:

  O loving God,
  spirit of consolation and giver of hope,
  we thank you for the gift of your faithful people who join us today.
  We ask you to bless and keep them in your care.
  Let us also pray for the souls of our departed loved ones.
  (Name your beloved and pause while others name theirs.)
  May perpetual light shine upon them and bring eternal rest.
  We ask this through Christ our Lord.
  Amen. *(Make the Sign of the Cross.)*

- Wish everyone well.

5. Fellowship Break (On-site 30 minutes)

Schedule as desired: before the session begins, before faith sharing, or as a finale.

Appendix

Sample Brochure (trifold template front)

A Christ-centered group is for you if any of these statements are true:

- You are looking for friends in Christ to share your journey of sorrow.
- You've been trying to figure out the meaning of your grief.
- You want to get on with life but haven't been able to.
- You find comfort in the teachings of Christ.
- You are open to new ways of coping with your grief.
- You don't want to feel alone anymore.

Adapted from

Seasons of Hope Leader's Guide: Bringing Comfort through Catholic Grief Support

Seasons of Hope

The Parish of

Sacred Heart Church

in Brockton, IL,

offers

Grief-Support Groups for Those Who Mourn

Come and Be Comforted!

Sample Brochure (trifold template back)

Parish Support for Adults Who Mourn

Our Lord assured us that those who mourn are blessed and that they shall be comforted. Seasons of Hope helps us come together to share in God's love. With the support of our faith community, we give voice to our unique journeys of grief and find healing and spiritual growth. Seasons of Hope is centered on Jesus Christ and grounded in the healing wisdom, traditions, and practices of the Catholic Church. It has four stand-alone, six-week seasons and journals that explore mourning through scripture, prayer, reflection activities, and faith sharing. Participating in all four seasons is a popular option but is not required.

Whether your loss is recent or long ago, if you are searching for our Lord in the midst of your grief, Seasons of Hope can help. It is a nurturing link to the Church, the Almighty, and people of faith who truly understand what it means to be brokenhearted.

Come and be comforted!

Fall 2023
Sacred Heart Parish

Seasons of Hope

Seasons of Hope
Grief Support Group
will meet on Saturdays
from
9:30 to 11:30 a.m.
October 7 to November
11
at the Parish Center.

For more information
and to save your spot,
contact
Mary Davis at
555-XXX-XXX
or *(email address)*
by October 4.

What Participants Say about Seasons of Hope

"I have really enjoyed this season, and I feel it has helped me go on."

"Seasons of Hope was what I needed. Although I have pain, the love and support helped me find joy in Christ and his Word. And I'm blessed with many new friends."

"Thank you so much for these Seasons of Hope sessions. They have meant more than you will ever know."

"Seasons of Hope's focus on prayer, scripture, and God helps each and every one of us to know that God loves us so much and that eternal life is a gift from him."

"I find our faith sharing inspirational. When people share from the heart, I feel it is the glue that helps heal my broken heart."

"I tried many bereavement groups. They were good, but something was missing. I knew it was God. When Seasons of Hope began here, it was the answer to my prayers."

APPENDIX

1. Season One Sessions-at-a-Glance

Session	Theme	Opening	Activity	Faith Sharing	Summary/Fellowship
1. Point of Departure	For Whom Are You Looking?	20 minutes	20 minutes Jn 20:11–18 Get to know one another.	35 minutes Linking loss to the emotions of the saints	5 minutes 30 minutes on-site
2. Path to Understanding	Our Source of Consolation	20 minutes	20 minutes Mt 11:28–30 Music: "My Yoke Is Easy" List what makes you weary.	35 minutes How God lightens burdens	5 minutes 30 minutes on-site
3. Obstacles on the Journey	Shattered Dreams	20 minutes	15 minutes Jer 18:1–6 Music: "Abba Father" Consider God as a loving potter.	40 minutes Honoring emotions and dreams	5 minutes 30 minutes on-site
4. Path to Inner Healing	Finding Joy	20 minutes	20 minutes Jn 16:19–24 Write a letter to God to rekindle joy.	40 minutes What helps in tough times	5 minutes 30 minutes on-site
5. Way of Suffering	The Way of the Cross	20 minutes	20 minutes Lk 23:13–56 Music: *Maundy Thursday* or *Requiem* Contemplate Stations of the Cross.	45 minutes Experiencing the way of the Cross	5 minutes 30 minutes on-site
6. Final Destination	Untie Him	10 minutes	30 minutes Jn 11:1–44 Share pictures.	40 minutes Jesus and our ties to our departed	5 minutes (survey) 30 minutes on-site

2. Season Two Sessions-at-a-Glance

Session	Theme	Opening	Activity	Faith Sharing	Summary/Fellowship
1. Point of Departure	Remembering	20 minutes	20 minutes Lk 24:1–12 Connect past to present loss.	35 minutes Comparing reactions to scripture story	5 minutes 30 minutes on-site
2. Path to Understanding	Seeking Consolation	20 minutes	20 minutes Jn 5:1–9 Music: "Sacred Silence" or "Song over the Water" List what holds you back.	35 minutes What it takes to heal after loss	5 minutes 30 minutes on-site
3. Obstacles on the Journey	Stumbling Blocks	20 minutes	20 minutes Is 57:14–15 Select stones.	40 minutes Moving stones	5 minutes 30 minutes on-site
4. Path to Inner Healing	Living Hope	20 minutes	20 minutes 1 Pt 1:3–9 **On-site:** Hand grief to Jesus. **Online:** Guided imagery and music: "Pachelbel' s Canon"	45 minutes What sustains hope	5 minutes 30 minutes on-site
5. Way of Suffering	The Cross	15 minutes	15 minutes Lk 9:22–24 Music: *Mater Eucharistiae* or *Benedicta* Meditation: rosary crucifix.	50 minutes Experiencing the Cross	5 minutes 30 minutes on-site
6. Final Destination	Do Not Be Afraid	10 minutes	25 minutes Lk 8:40–42, 49–56 Share memories.	35 minutes Inviting Jesus in	15 minutes (survey) 30 minutes on-site

3. Season Three Sessions-at-a-Glance

Session	Theme	Opening	Activity	Faith Sharing	Summary/Fellowship
1. Point of Departure	Believing	20 minutes	20 minutes Jn 20:24–29 Get to know each other.	35 minutes Exploring reactions to loss	5 minutes 30 minutes on-site
2. Path to Understanding	Knock and the Door Shall Be Opened	20 minutes	20 minutes Mt 7:7–11 Draw picture. List what you need.	35 minutes Praying with confidence	5 minutes 30 minutes on-site
3. Obstacles on the Journey	Our Infirmities	20 minutes	20 minutes Lk 13:10–13 Music: "You Raise Me Up" Imagine how it will feel to have Jesus heal you.	40 minutes Being weighed down	5 minutes 30 minutes on-site
4. Path to Inner Healing	Blinders to Faith	20 minutes	15 minutes Lk 18:35–43 Letter of petition to God	45 minutes Persevering in faith	5 minutes 30 minutes on-site
5. Way of Suffering	His Wound of Love	15 minutes	15 minutes 1 Pt 2:20b–24 Music: *Maundy Thursday* or *Requiem* Meditation: Sacred Heart of Jesus	45 minutes Being touched by love	5 minutes 30 minutes on-site
6. Final Destination	Do Not Weep	10 minutes	30 minutes Lk 7:11–17 Share faith symbols.	40 minutes Drying the tears	15 minutes (survey) 30 minutes on-site

APPENDIX

4. Season Four Sessions-at-a-Glance

Session	Theme	Opening	Activity	Faith Sharing	Summary/Fellowship
1. Point of Departure	Last Encounter	20 minutes	20 minutes Jn 14:1–8 Get to know each other.	35 minutes Linking faith with coping	5 minutes 30 minutes on-site
2. Path to Understanding	The Garden of Gethsemane	20 minutes	15 minutes Mk 14:32–42 Music: *Requiem* List your requests.	40 minutes Seeking answers to prayer	5 minutes 30 minutes on-site
3. Obstacles on the Journey	Crown of Thorns	20 minutes	15 minutes Jn 19:1–3 Write what eased your spiritual thorn.	45 minutes Finding roses among the thorns	5 minutes 30 minutes on-site
4. Path to Inner Healing	Gift of Caring	15 minutes	20 minutes Jn 19:25–30 Letter of gratitude to God.	40 minutes Exploring the healing power of kindness	5 minutes 30 minutes on-site
5. Way of Suffering	Why Have You Forsaken Me?	15 minutes	20 minutes Mk 15:22–34 Meditation: Divine Mercy	45 minutes Approaching the fountain of grace and mercy	5 minutes 30 minutes on-site
6. Final Destination	Be My Witnesses	10 minutes	35 minutes Acts 1:6–11 Share a symbol of love.	40 minutes Bearing witness	15 minutes (survey) 30 minutes on-site

1. Season One *Journal*-at-a-Glance

Session	Theme	Scriptural Focus	Reflection	Journal Entry	Moving Forward
1. Point of Departure	*Why Are You Weeping?*	Jn 20:11–18 Meaning of loss	Uses photo of happier time to focus on positive emotion.	Thinks of tomb scene. Writes to Jesus about grief.	Lights a candle for the deceased.
2. Path to Understanding	Our Source of Consolation	Mt 11:28–30 Jesus and funeral as comfort	Remembers who/what lightened the burden at wake or funeral.	Dialogues with God about current burden.	Reaches out to someone.
3. Obstacles on the Journey	Picking Up the Pieces	Jer 18:1–6 The Potter's hand in grief	Imagines a shattered pot and if it can be fixed.	Describes brokenhearted feelings and seeks Jesus.	Spends time before the Blessed Sacrament.
4. Path to Inner Healing	Finding Joy	Jn 16:19–24 Weeping and mourning become joy	Thinks of joy before loss and whether God was included.	Notes how deceased gave joy and impacted life.	Rejoices about something this week.
5. Way of Suffering	Bearing Your Cross	Lk 23:13–56 The Cross of Christ	Gazes on a cross and ponders its meaning to the deceased and self.	Shares own experiences stumbling and falling with the cross of mourning.	Thinks about each word and motion during the Sign of the Cross.
6. Final Destination	Letting God	Jn 11:1–44 Martha's handling of death; Jesus's teaching	Contemplates Jesus's tears.	Lists complaints and searches for the glory of God in losing someone.	Prays with incense.

2. Season Two *Journal*-at-a-Glance

Session	Theme	Scriptural Focus	Reflection	Journal Entry	Moving Forward
1. Point of Departure	Disbelief	Lk 24:1–12 The unexpected	Looks at memento of the deceased and focuses on positive emotion.	Reviews how apostles reacted and writes to Jesus about own disbelief.	Places memento with picture of deceased and offers a prayer.
2. Path to Understanding	Seeking Consolation	Jn 5:1–9 Taking up your mat	Considers own grief journey.	Dialogues with God about motivators to action.	Prays for those who have helped.
3. Obstacles on the Journey	Stones for Building	Is 57:14–15 Stones of life.	Examines boulders on the path to healing.	Writes about being crushed in spirit.	Blesses and carries a stone this week.
4. Path to Inner Healing	Living Hope	1 Pt 1:3–9 Our inheritance	Probes whether good can come from trials.	Notes when hope entered own grief.	Encourages someone.
5. Way of Suffering	Sorrow	Lk 9:22–24 The Passion' s meaning	Imagines Mary's sorrow as Jesus carried the Cross.	Shares own sorrow.	Prays the Sorrowful Mysteries.
6. Final Destination	Just Have Faith	Lk 8:40–42, 49–56 Faith saves	Recalls bringing Jesus to the beloved.	Thanks Jesus for his help.	Kneels at the tabernacle to pray.

3. Season Three *Journal*-at-a-Glance

Session	Theme	Scriptural Focus	Reflection	Journal Entry	Moving Forward
1. Point of Departure	Doubting Thomas	Jn 20:24–29 The encounter with Jesus	Contemplates the sacred wounds.	Writes thoughts about life after death.	Visits the beloved's final resting place.
2. Path to Understanding	Open Doors	Mt 7:7–11 Prayerful asking	Considers what God's will might be regarding grief.	Dialogues with Jesus about trust.	In prayer, beholds the doors of the tabernacle.
3. Obstacles on the Journey	Crippled Spirit	Lk 13:10–13 Bent with worry	Recognizes God's helping hand in mourning.	Confides troubles.	Seeks the Sacrament of Reconciliation.
4. Path to Inner Healing	Blind Faith	Lk 18:35–43 Jesus's compassion	Asks if Jesus's pity has been sought.	Tells Jesus how to help with grief.	Helps someone who needs compassion.
5. Way of Suffering	Christ's Example	1 Pt 2:20b–24 Jesus's footsteps	Explores how the deceased's life reflected God.	Shares trying to follow the Lord.	Asks for courage while receiving the Eucharist this week.
6. Final Destination	No Tears	Lk 7:11–17 The mercy of Jesus	Recalls the funeral procession of the beloved.	Acknowledges how Jesus touches grief.	Arranges a memorial Mass.

4. Season Four *Journal*-at-a-Glance

Session	Theme	Scriptural Focus	Reflection	Journal Entry	Moving Forward
1. Point of Departure	The Father's House	Jn 14:1–8 Grasping the truth	Contemplates heaven.	Writes about being left behind.	Uses centering prayer.
2. Path to Understanding	Betrayal	Mk 14:32–42 Keeping watch	Reviews the positive support given to a loved one.	Shares a difficult moment with the deceased.	Genuflects mindfully.
3. Obstacles on the Journey	Suffering	Jn 19:1–3 Injury	Considers the resurrected Christ.	Considers how suffering through grief transforms.	Receives Communion from the cup.
4. Path to Inner Healing	Infinite Thirst	Jn 19:25–30 Love	Focuses on the compassion of Christ.	Explores responding to Jesus's thirst for love	Reaches out to someone in mourning.
5. Way of Suffering	Hurtful Words	Mk 15:22–34 Jesus as victim	Ponders the power of words.	Lifts up wounded feelings to the Lord.	Praises the Lord.
6. Final Destination	Patience	Acts 1:6–11 Waiting for the kingdom	Explores attitude toward patience.	Tells Jesus what is hoped for now.	Prays the Glorious Mysteries of the Rosary.

Suggested Sound Recordings and Sacred Images

Pre-session Instrumental Music

Briggs, Tami. *Touched by Angels*. Musical Reflections, https://musicalreflections.com.

Haugen, Marty. *Instruments of Peace*. GIA Publications, www.giamusic.com.

Schutte, Dan. *You Are Near*. Oregon Catholic Press, www.ocp.org.

Talbot, John Michael. *Quiet Pathways*. Apple Music, https://music.apple.com/us/album/quiet-pathways/76077804.

Session Music and Sacred Images

Season One

Session 2:

Talbot, John Michael. *Master Collection V.I: The Quiet Side*. Sparrow Corporation, https://troubadourforthelord.net.

Session 3:

Landry, Carey. *Abba, Father: Prayer Songs of Rev. Carey Landry*. Oregon Catholic Press, www.ocp.org.

Session 5:

Monastic Choir of St. Peter's Abbey of Solesmes, France. *Maundy Thursday: Gregorian Chant*. Creative Joys, https://paracletepress.com.

Priestly Fraternity of St. Peter. *Requiem*. Sony Classical, www.vaultrecordings.com.

Stations of the Cross images—https://aleteia.org/slideshow/pray-the-stations-of-the-cross-with-these-beautiful-images-and-prayers-1374.

Season Two

Session 2:

Booth, Tom. *Unravel*. Oregon Catholic Press, www.ocp.org.

Haugen, Marty. *Anthology II: 1985–1989*. GIA Publications, www.giamusic.com.

Session 4:

Kobialka, Daniel. *Timeless Motion*. Li-Sem Enterprises.

Session 5:

Dominican Sisters of Mary, Mother of the Eucharist. *Mater Eucharistiae*. Decca Label Group, www.openlightmedia.com.

Monks of Norcia. *Benedicta: Marian Chant from Norcia*. Sophia Institute Press, https://sophiamusicgroup.com.

Season Three

Session 3:

Groban, Josh. *Closer*. 143 Reprise Records.

Session 5:

Monastic Choir of St. Peter's Abbey of Solesmes, France. *Maundy Thursday: Gregorian Chant*. Creative Joys, https://paracletepress.com.

Priestly Fraternity of St. Peter. *Requiem*. Sony Classical, www.vaultrecordings.com.

Sacred Heart of Jesus image. https://m.theholyrosary.org/sacredheart/.

Season Four

Session 2:

Priestly Fraternity of St. Peter's Choir. *Requiem*. Sony Classical, www.vaultrecordings.com.

Session 5:

Divine Mercy image. www.thedivinemercy.org/message.

Helpful Resources for the Team

Books

DeLorenzo, Leonard J. *Our Faithful Departed: Where They Are and Why It Matters*. Notre Dame, IN: Ave Maria Press, 2022.

Do Something Beautiful for God: The Essential Teachings of Mother Teresa: 365 Daily Reflections. Introduction by Matthew Kelly. North Palm Beach, FL: Blue Sparrow, 2019.

Jones, Laurie Beth. *Jesus, CEO: Using Ancient Wisdom for Visionary Leadership (25th Anniversary Edition)*. New York: Hachette Go, 2021.

Kübler-Ross, Elisabeth, and David Kessler. *On Grief and Grieving: Finding the Meaning of Grief through the Five Stages of Loss*. New York: Scribner, 2005.

Noel, Brook, and Pamela D. Blair. *I Wasn't Ready to Say Goodbye: Surviving, Coping, and Healing after the Sudden Death of a Loved One*. Updated ed. Naperville, IL: Sourcebooks, 2008.

Nouwen, Henri J. M. *The Wounded Healer: Ministry in Contemporary Society*. New York: Image, 1979.

———. *Turn My Mourning into Dancing: Finding Hope in Hard Times*. Nashville: Thomas Nelson, 2001.

O'Connor, Mary-Frances. *The Grieving Brain: The Surprising Science of How We Learn from Love and Loss*. New York: Harper One, 2022.

O'Hearn, Patrick, Bryan Feger, Ryan Breaux, and Red Bird Ministry. *The Grief of Dads: Support and Hope for Catholic Fathers Navigating Child Loss*. Notre Dame, IN: Ave Maria Press, 2023.

Pitre, Brant. *Jesus and the Jewish Roots of Mary: Unveiling the Mother of the Messiah*. New York: Image, 2018.

Pope Francis. *On Faith*. Chicago: Loyola Press, 2019.

———. *On Hope*. Chicago: Loyola Press, 2018.

Rupp, Joyce. *Boundless Compassion: Creating a Way of Life*. Notre Dame, IN: Sorin, 2018.

———. *Now That You've Gone Home: Courage and Comfort for Times of Grief*. Notre Dame, IN: Ave Maria Press, 2009.

Shoener, Ed, and John P. Dolan, eds. *Responding to Suicide: A Pastoral Handbook for Catholic Leaders*. Notre Dame, IN: Ave Maria Press, 2020.

Sullender, R. Scott. *Trauma and Grief: Resources and Strategies for Ministry*. Eugene, OR: Cascade Books, 2018.

Tighe, Tommy. *St. Dymphna's Playbook: A Catholic Guide to Finding Mental and Emotional Well-Being*. Notre Dame, IN: Ave Maria Press, 2021.

Van Zeller, Hubert. *The Mystery of Suffering: A Spiritual Classic on Trust in Divine Providence*. Notre Dame, IN: Christian Classics, 2015.

White, Michael, and Tom Corcoran. *Seriously, God? Making Sense of Life Not Making Sense.* Notre Dame, IN: Ave Maria Press, 2021.

Also see the appendix of any Seasons of Hope *Journal* for books on grieving the loss of loved ones.

Websites

https://bible.usccb.org/bible provides free access to the New American Bible.

www.avemariapress.com/products/seasons-of-hope-facilitators-pack provides Seasons of Hope books, logo, pdfs, survey, as well as webinars and videos for facilitator enrichment that build upon the spiritual and practical advice in this *Leader's Guide.*

Special Grief Situations

www.hopeafterabortion.com connects to Project Rachel Ministry, which helps those who want post-abortion support and those who provide it.

www.hospicefoundation.org offers useful information on many facets of the grief journey.

www.pomc.org (Parents of Murdered Children) provides information, grief support, and help with the criminal system to survivors of homicide victims.

www.samhsa.gov (Substance Abuse and Mental Health Services Administration) has fact sheets with tips for survivors coping with grief after a disaster, traumatic event, community violence, or COVID-19 death.

www.whatsyourgrief.com offers booklets, courses, podcasts, and webinars on grief and loss, grief support, and coping with grief for adults, teens, and children.

www.avemariapress.com/spotlight/podcast-shoener presents Deacon Ed Shoener's talk "A Catholic Response to Talking About Suicide."

www.compassionatefriends.org offers local peer support for families experiencing the death of a child, as well as information on grieving and links to related organizations.

www.dougy.org (The Dougy Center) offers support for grieving children and families, plus grief resources, toolkits, podcasts, books, and webinars.

www.elizabethministry.com has resources that bring hope, help, and healing to those grieving from miscarriage or infant or child death.

www.grasphelp.org offers support groups and resources for those who lose a loved one through addiction and overdose in the United States and Canada.

www.healgrief.org provides tools to find secular local and national support, plus grief resources, virtual groups, and educational programs.

www.samaritanshope.org offers suicide-survivor information for adults, teens, and children, plus community education and outreach.

www.taps.org links those grieving the death of a military loved one to free grief resources, including casework, counseling, publications, retreats, and seminars.

Referral for Professional Grief Support

Diocesan branches of Catholic Charities and Catholic Social Services often provide counseling for people experiencing depression, anxiety, or a traumatic loss.

Hospice programs that provide Medicare services to families offer a variety of professional bereavement support options, up to a year following their loss.

www.catholicmhm.org provides a list of helpful organizations identified by the Association of Catholic Mental Health Ministers.

www.catholictherapists.com lists therapists committed to Church teachings.

Note: Updates to Helpful Resources for the Team will be posted at avemariapress.com as needed.

M. Donna MacLeod is a Catholic lay leader and founder of the Seasons of Hope ministry to the bereaved. She is the author of the program's bestselling leader's guide, four journals, and digital support resources. This work was inspired by the death of her youngest daughter, Erynne, in 1988 and the compassionate response of MacLeod's parish to the loss.

MacLeod holds bachelor's and master's degrees in nursing and has served as an oncology clinical specialist, nurse educator, administrator, and hospice professional.

She presents keynote addresses, workshops, retreats, and other events online and at numerous national and diocesan conferences and parish events related to grief, loss, and ministry leadership in the United States and Canada.

An experienced mentor, MacLeod supports Seasons of Hope facilitators with an online enrichment series sponsored by Ave Maria Press, and leads parish groups in the Diocese of Fall River. She served on the board of trustees and train-the-trainer faculty of the former National Catholic Ministry to the Bereaved and is a member of the Catholic Family Life Association.

MacLeod lives with her husband, Bryan, in the Boston, Massachusetts, area. She can be reached at seasonsofhope35@gmail.com.

Most Rev. John P. Dolan is the bishop of the Diocese of Phoenix. Ordained to the priesthood in 1989, Dolan previously served as auxiliary bishop of San Diego from 2017 to 2022.

GET THE PARTICIPANT JOURNALS

The program contains four journals that can be used by individuals for spiritual reflection and prayer or by parish bereavement groups who are following the *Seasons of Hope Leader's Guide*. You can start with any of the four journals since the seasons are not sequential.

The journals, originally published in 2007, have been revised with a new introduction and updated resource listings. The journals also include Bible references, reflections, faith-sharing questions, prayers, and space for writing.

EACH JOURNAL COVERS A UNIQUE, STANDALONE "SEASON" OF SIX SESSIONS THAT HAVE THEIR OWN THEME.

Journal One themes include

- For whom are you looking?
- Our source of consolation
- Shattered dreams
- Finding joy
- The Way of the Cross
- Untie him

Journal Two themes include

- Remembering
- Seeking consolation
- Stumbling blocks
- Living hope
- The Cross
- Do not be afraid

Journal Three themes include

- Believing
- Knock and the door shall be opened
- Our infirmities
- Blinders to faith
- His wounds
- Do not weep

Journal Four themes include

- Last encounter
- The Garden of Gethsemane
- Crown of Thorns
- Gift of caring
- Golgotha
- Be my witnesses